Metropolitan Reform in St. Louis

HENRY J. SCHMANDT,
UNIVERSITY OF WISCONSIN (MILWAUKEE) ·
PAUL G. STEINBICKER, ST. LOUIS UNI-
VERSITY · GEORGE D. WENDEL, ST. LOUIS
UNIVERSITY

A Case Study

HOLT, RINEHART AND WINSTON, NEW YORK

*Metropolitan
Reform in
St. Louis*

Foreword

Metropolitan communities will be wrestling with governmental complexity and the ills that flow therefrom for many years to come.

This brief account of an unsuccessful effort to solve what disinterested analysts (but not, apparently, a majority of the citizens) perceived as urgent metropolitan problems in the St. Louis area may help others to achieve success. By clear implication, at least, it indicates some or most of the conditions that must ordinarily exist if major governmental changes are to win popular approval.

Though the plan for a metropolitan government was defeated, other aspects of the Metropolitan St. Louis Survey's report, not dealt with here, remain very much alive. At this writing, for example, a constitutional amendment has been proposed that to a considerable degree follows the report's recommendations for strengthening the county government's powers. And even the losing fight was worth waging. It broke new ground in research; it focused attention on local issues that will become steadily more urgent; and it taught some valuable lessons to all who want the metropolitan communities of the United States efficiently organized for healthy development.

THOMAS H. ELIOT
PAUL G. STEINBICKER

Codirectors,
Metropolitan St. Louis Survey

v

Preface

On November 3, 1959 voters of St. Louis City and St. Louis County decisively rejected a proposed plan to establish a metropolitan governmental agency to be known as the "Greater St. Louis City-County District." The referendum followed a comprehensive survey of the area's governmental problems by the two local universities, St. Louis and Washington, and a year's work and deliberation by a board of freeholders. Defeat of the proposal came as no great surprise to the hardened observer cognizant of the long history of failure to achieve metropolitan governmental reorganization. Yet here was a large-scale effort to attack the growing inadequacies of the local governmental pattern in one of the nation's major metropolises—an effort that involved substantial time, funds, and human resources. Why did it fail?

Simply stated, the present case study is an attempt to answer this question. After examining the background of the reorganization movement and the general setting in which it operated, the study concentrates on the work of the Metropolitan Board of Freeholders, the results of the deliberations of this body, and the campaign for adoption of the proposed plan. In this way the case study seeks to identify and analyze the significant forces that came into operation over the reorganization issue. Finally, the study advances certain conclusions in order to explain the failure of the St. Louis movement and offers a number of generalizations relating to metropolitan reform efforts.

We are especially grateful to the Ford Foundation for the grant which made this study possible. We are also deeply indebted to Thomas H. Eliot and Carl McCandless, both of Washington University, who read the manuscript and who made many valuable suggestions. Their knowledge of the local political scene and of the events which transpired during the period covered by this study is intimate and extensive. Our thanks also go to J. Terence Manns, now of the University of Houston, who served as administrative assistant to the Metropolitan Board of Freeholders and who generously assisted us in assembling and interpreting the data. Others such as Scott Greer, of Northwestern University, and John C. Bollens, of the University of California at Los Angeles, contributed greatly to our understanding of metropolitan communities. Errors of fact or interpretation are, of course, our sole responsibility.

HENRY J. SCHMANDT
PAUL G. STEINBICKER
GEORGE DORIAN WENDEL

St. Louis, Missouri

Contents

Tables

Metropolitan
Reform in
St. Louis

ONE

The Setting

Every reform movement is shaped in varying degrees by its temporal and spatial environment. The present metropolitan experiment is no exception. From the beginning its course was greatly influenced by the setting and climate. Tradition, past events, personalities, the general temper of the period, and local peculiarities affected in one fashion or another the action movement and its results. A brief description of this environmental background thus becomes a necessary prelude to the case study.

PHYSICAL AND DEMOGRAPHIC CHARACTERISTICS

Situated in the heart of the Midwest at the confluence of two of the nation's great rivers, Missouri and Mississippi, metropolitan St. Louis has long enjoyed strong if not spectacular growth. Over two million people now reside within its census-defined Standard Metropolitan Statistical Area, an area that includes in addition to St. Louis City and St. Louis County two other counties in Missouri and two in Illinois. Approximately 1.5 million live in St. Louis City and County, the locale of this study. Dissatisfaction with the county government led St. Louisans to detach their territory from the county in 1876—an event that froze the city's boundaries in perpetuity and placed the growing core of the metropolis in a confining and enduring strait jacket.

St. Louis City, its 61 square miles shaped like a half moon, is surrounded by the county on the north, south, and west and the Mississippi River on the east. Although the city is an old and built-up community, a vigorous redevelopment program of recent years has cleared out large sections of slums in the interior,

1

but as the latest census revealed, the process of renewal has also contributed to a decline of over 100,000 in its population (from 856,796 to 750,021) during the decade. In contrast, St. Louis County with 497 square miles of territory, less than one half of it developed, has more than tripled in population since 1930 until it now contains approximately 700,000 residents.

The city's most urgent problems involve blight and decay, congestion, and acculturation of its newcomers; the county's most pressing needs are new and enlarged public services and facilities, new schools, new industry and commerce to balance its tax base, and better planning for orderly expansion. The central city constitutes the commercial and industrial core of the area, although large business agglomerations and industrial establishments are becoming more commonplace in the suburbs. At present somewhat over 50 percent of employed county residents work in the core city.

Typical of many other northern and Midwestern manufacturing centers, St. Louis has experienced a large in-migration of low-income workers during recent decades. As a consequence, the city's population has come to include a disproportionate share of Negroes and the poorer dwellers of the area. Today approximately 30 percent of its residents are Negro. The county, with predominantly single-family units, many fine residential enclaves, and numerous neighborhoods of high social rank, has become a haven for those fleeing from the central city and for the new professional and managerial personnel moving into the area.

St. Louis County does not conform to the common image of suburbia with its white-Protestant-Republican triad. White it unmistakably is—its Negro population is quite small, although the expansion of Negro neighborhoods on the periphery of the central city is beginning to penetrate the county's borders—but conformity to the image vanishes at this point. Since World War II blue-collar workers, mostly craftsmen, have settled in large numbers in newly developed county communities, altering both the political and religious complexions of the area. Democrats, for example, now hold most of the county-wide elective offices and control the council. They do not, however, hold total predominance as in the city, the division between the political parties remaining fairly close. In addition, over 30 percent of county residents are Roman Catholics. This composition is reflected in the suburban Catholic school system with its 75 elementary and 14 high schools accommodating almost 50,000 pupils. So long as industrial expansion in suburbia continues, as it seems destined to do, the county's social, political, and religious characteristics will undergo further modifications.

THE GOVERNMENTAL PATTERN

St. Louis City is governed by a strong mayor-council form. Legislative powers are vested in a 29-member board of aldermen, with the president elected at large and other members by wards. All elections to city office are on a partisan basis. Mayor Raymond R. Tucker, a moderate Democrat and former university professor who won his first mayoralty nomination over strong opposition from the party organization, was serving his second term at the time of the action program. Highly respected, he has pushed broad programs of public and private development to "revitalize" the city. In these and other efforts he has enjoyed the strong support of the metropolitan press and the business leadership of the community, the latter symbolized by Civic Progress, Incorporated, a small group of economically dominant citizens.

Unlike the integrated governmental structure of the city, the county pattern is highly fragmented. In addition to the county government, there are 98 municipalities ranging in population from less than 50 to slightly over 50,000; 20 fire-protection districts; 27 individual school systems; and a county-wide school district for handicapped children. The county government has operated under a home-rule charter since 1950. Legislative authority rests in a council of seven members elected by districts. A supervisor chosen at large serves as executive head, sharing administrative responsibilities with several other elected officials. The position, however, has not attained high public stature, partly because of the circumscribed powers and partly because of the individuals who have occupied the office. All elections to county offices are on a partisan basis while those in the suburban municipalities are nonpartisan.

An exceptionally large number of suburbanites, over 175,000, live in unincorporated areas, many of which have taken on the characteristics of organized communities. The urban service needs of these areas are met in varying fashion by the county government, fire districts, the metropolitan sewer district, and private contractors. The county furnishes them with police protection, health and sanitation services, zoning control, subdivision regulation, building inspection, and road maintenance. Municipalities may contract for similar services but few have take any appreciable advantage of this opportunity except for their public health needs.

No formal cooperative agreements of any import exist between the city and local governments of the county. Suburban units have preferred to operate independently of their giant neighbor and to avoid any display of reliance on it for their service needs. The city, however, maintains many public facilities such as the art museum, zoo, and library reference rooms which are used extensively by county residents. In 1946 it levied an earnings tax of one half of 1 percent on all salaries and corporate profits earned within its boundaries. This tax, which affects the many county residents who work in St. Louis, was raised to 1 percent in 1959, an increase that took effect only three months before the election on the metropolitan charter, obviously not endearing the city to its suburban relatives.

PRIOR EFFORTS AT REORGANIZATION

Attempts to achieve metropolitan governmental reform in St. Louis have a long history. Less than a half century after the city was separated from the county, population growth and its concomitant problems set in motion a long chain of efforts to adjust relations between the two jurisdictions. In 1926 residents of the area were presented with a plan for total consolidation of all local units of government. Voters in the city favored the proposal by a seven to one majority; those in the suburbs rejected it by a margin of more than two to one. Since separate majorities were required in each area, the reorganization effort failed.

A second major attempt took place in 1930 when local groups, spearheaded by the chamber of commerce, endeavored to secure constitutional authorization for a plan to establish a federation of local governments. After a vigorous campaign, the proposed enabling amendment narrowly passed in the central city but lost decisively in the county and state as a whole. Significantly, the city administration opposed the amendment, contending that federation would impose excessive obligations on St. Louis taxpayers.

After 1950 and prior to the present metropolitan experiment, two attempts were made to adjust city-county relations on a more moderate basis than the earlier plans envisaged. The first, to create an integrated sewer system for the city and the urbanized portion of the county, was approved by popular referendum in 1954. The second, to establish an area-wide transit authority, was rejected by voters of both jurisdictions in 1955.

The defeat of the transit plan led to demands by the metropolitan press and civic groups for a comprehensive transportation survey. In calling for such a study, they pointed out that formulation of the sewer district charter had been preceded by careful examination and analysis of the area's sewage problems while the transit proposal had been drafted and presented to the voters without benefit of prior systematic study. As a result of this agitation, a committee of six members was appointed by the mayor of St. Louis and the county supervisor to prepare specifications for a major transportation study and to supervise its execution. Financed by city, county, state, and federal funds, the survey began in 1956 and was completed in August 1959, two months before the election on the metropolitan district proposal.[1]

While plans for the transit study were under way, another movement originated that was destined to have wide repercussions on the future course of governmental reorganization efforts in the St. Louis area. Led by A. J. Cervantes,

[1] Analyses of the transit study are contained in R. Gilman Smith, "Co-ordinated Transport Planning for the St. Louis Area," *Traffic Quarterly*, April 1960, and Henry J. Schmandt, "Efficiency of Movement: A Facet of the Metropolitan Problem," *Traffic Quarterly*, June 1960.

a young, energetic, and politically ambitious St. Louis alderman, a group known as the Citizens Committee for City-County Co-ordination was organized to campaign for a metropolitan charter. Cervantes explained the origin of the movement in this way:

Serving as Alderman of the Fifteenth Ward and as Chairman of the Traffic Committee of the Board of Aldermen, we were confronted with many traffic problems not only in the City, but as it reached the County line. Many other mutual problems repeatedly came to my attention. In February of 1955 I advocated that a six or eight man board be set up between the City and County to work out our mutual problem and as I was drafting a resolution, a City Hall reporter said that the 1945 Constitution had set up machinery for just this. He showed me the Section and Article and, as candidate for the President of the Board of Aldermen, this was included in my platform.[2]

The constitutional provision to which Cervantes referred—a provision that had been previously employed in the formation of the sewer district and in the abortive attempt to create a transit authority—establishes a mechanism for adjusting city-county relations.[3] Under its terms a metropolitan board of free-holders must be appointed upon petition by registered voters of the city and county equal in number to 3 percent of the last gubernatorial vote cast in each of the two jurisdictions. This board must then draft and present to the voters a reorganization plan based on one of four alternative approaches:

1. Merger of all city and county governments into one municipal government of the City of St. Louis;
2. Reentry of the city into the county;
3. Enlargement of the boundaries of the city by annexing county territory;
4. Creation of a metropolitan district or districts for the administration of services common to the area.

Cervantes enlisted the assistance of an able young lawyer, H. Jackson Daniel, who was active in Democratic politics in St. Louis County, and the two organized a group of some 50 individuals, heavily weighted with lawyers and union representatives. In June 1955 the committee began an extensive campaign to collect signatures for the appointment of a freeholders' board.

From the beginning the committee labored under a cloud of "political taint." In many circles the group was believed to be politically motivated because of its leadership under two active Democrats and its backing by a number of labor leaders. Mayor Tucker denounced the movement as premature and warned against hasty efforts in arriving at solutions to the area's problems.[4] Tucker, obviously irked at Cervantes, viewed the movement as a political vehicle for

2 Transcript of meeting of Metropolitan Board of Freeholders, July 1, 1958.
3 Missouri Constitution, 1945, Art. VI, Sec. 30.
4 *St. Louis Post-Dispatch,* October 20, 1955.

furthering the latter's well-known mayoralty ambitions. Top business and community leaders, taking their cue from Tucker, refused to be coopted into the movement or to assist it financially. As a consequence, the citizens committee never attained high civic stature but remained somewhat suspect throughout its existence.

METROPOLITAN ST. LOUIS SURVEY

During the period of metropolitan reorganization activity in the middle fifties—first with the sewer district, later with the transit proposal and its aftermath—members of the political science departments at St. Louis University and Washington University had informally explored the possibility of conducting a broad-scaled examination of the area's governmental problems. As a result of these discussions, the two universities made a joint application to the Ford Foundation for funds to undertake such a study. The filing of the application came at a time when the citizens committee was instituting its initial campaign to secure petition signatures.

When Mayor Tucker learned of the university application he immediately saw in it the answer to the problem posed by the Cervantes movement. Publicly expressing approval of such a study, he set about generating interest among business and civic leaders of the community. Largely through his efforts a local foundation, the McDonnell Aircraft Corporation Charitable Trust, indicated willingness to contribute $50,000 toward the project. County leaders, including Supervisor Luman Matthews, also endorsed the study. Many of those who extolled its merits pointed to the necessity of an objective and professional survey of the area's needs and problems before jumping precipitously into the drafting of official reorganization plans. In support of this position they cited the contrasting experiences of the sewer and transit plans.

How much of the interest displayed in the proposed study was genuine and how much prompted by the desire to deflate the activity of the citizens committee and ward off the immediate appointment of a board of freeholders can only be speculated upon. Suffice it to say, the citizens committee found itself in the unenviable position of pushing for immediate action while the top political and business leadership of the community was maintaining that the university study should in all good sense precede official charter drafting. Convinced of the futility of continuing in the face of opposition from this impressive combination, leaders of the citizens committee agreed to delay their signature-gathering campaign and join in endorsing the proposed study. This somewhat incongruous but united front of community leadership with its avowed demonstration of interest in reorganization was a persuasive factor in the decision of the Ford Foundation to make its first grant in the urban-metropolitan field.

Known as the Metropolitan St. Louis Survey, the university study began in the summer of 1956 financed by the Ford Foundation grant of $250,000 and the McDonnell award of $50,000. Over-all responsibility for the survey was placed in a board of control consisting of the heads of the two universities (who played only nominal roles), the chairmen of the two political science departments, and an executive officer appointed by the board to serve as research director. The board had complete freedom in designing the study and formulating recommendations. At no time during the course of its work was it subjected to any outside pressures. No citizens committee of an advisory or other nature participated formally in the survey's work or reviewed the recommendations before their release to the public.

The survey was under only one pressure, time. In acquiescing in the study approach, the citizens committee indicated that it could not prolong the filing of petitions much beyond one year because a longer period might invalidate the many signatures already collected. With time as an important factor, the work was planned for completion in late summer of 1957, a deadline that was met. As one who participated in the project has noted, the survey "probably had the largest budget and most ambitious agenda for the shortest period of operating time ever allowed a study of metropolitan government." [5]

The study was broadly designed to include an examination of social and economic factors as well as organizational and service problems on the premise that metropolitan reform cannot be oblivious to the total environment in which local government operates. Included in the survey's work, for example, was a citizens' attitude and participation study that involved extensive interviews with more than 2,000 city and county residents and an economic base study that enlisted the active cooperation and assistance of the area's major industries.[6]

The survey issued two public reports, *Background for Action* and *Path of Progress.*[7] The first was a factual inventory of the area's social and economic characteristics and its local governments; the second contained a series of recommendations relating to governmental reorganization. The principal proposal called for the establishment of an area-wide government with jurisdiction over certain common functions. Others related to school district financing and consolidation, merging of smaller municipalities, and strengthening county government. No over-all solution that could be accomplished in a single action, such as complete consolidation of existing governmental units, was proposed. The major recommendation could be effected by action of a board of freeholders and

[5] Scott Greer, "Dilemmas of Action Research on the Metropolitan Problem," in *Community Political Systems*, Morris Janowitz, ed., New York: The Free Press of Glencoe, Inc., 1961, p. 190.

[6] A detailed description of these studies and the other work of the survey is contained in John C. Bollens, ed., *Exploring the Metropolitan Community*, Berkeley, Calif.: University of California Press, 1961.

[7] St. Louis: Metropolitan St. Louis Survey, February 1957 and August 1957.

popular acceptance while the others required county charter amendment or state legislative and constitutional modification. Important as these latter recommendations may have been, the metropolitan government proposal constituted the heart of the report, and it was over this that the ensuing civic battle was waged.

SURVEY RECOMMENDATIONS

The survey recommendations for a metropolitan district government are summarized here because they became the focal point of debate in the charter-drafting and action phases that followed completion of the study.

Under the survey's proposals, a metropolitan government in the form of a multifunctional special district would be established for the St. Louis City–St. Louis County area. No existing local governmental unit, whether a municipality or school district, would lose its legal autonomy under the plan. Only the metropolitan sewer district would be affected because its functions would be absorbed by the new government. Legislative authority of the metropolitan agency would be vested in a council of 14 members, 12 popularly elected and one each appointed by the mayor of St. Louis and the county supervisor. Three of the St. Louis representatives would be chosen in city-wide elections, three of the suburban members by county-wide vote, and the other six by district balloting. A chief executive, to be known as president, would be chosen at large by the voters of the area. All elections would be on a nonpartisan basis.

The new government would have power to:

1. Establish a metropolitan road system by designating and controlling arterial highways and streets (this function including construction and maintenance of arterial roads, traffic control, and regulation or operation of off-street parking facilities);

2. Assume regulatory power over all local mass-transit facilities, and if necessary, acquire and operate a mass-transit system;

3. Prepare and adopt a comprehensive master plan of development for the entire area and require local zoning ordinances to conform substantially to the plan;

4. Acquire, assemble, and develop industrial and commercial tracts of land for lease or sale to private persons or corporations for manufacturing and business purposes;

5. Take over the functions of the existing Metropolitan St. Louis Sewer District;

6. Assume all civil defense responsibilities of the local units in the area;

7. Take over all property assessment functions in the city and county.

These recommendations embody the principles of local federalism. Functions of common public concern that cannot be handled satisfactorily within the existing system of local government are transferred to an agency with area-wide jurisdiction; all others are retained by the individual local units. In drafting the proposals, the survey endeavored to eschew what appeared totally impractical from the standpoint of political reality and to offer instead meritorious solutions with chance of popular acceptance. As one of the group's directors expressed it, "The Survey's members weighed the urgency of change against the difficulties of achieving it, and agreed on that course which seemed to them necessary and reasonably possible of acceptance."[8] For this purpose they relied heavily on the findings of the sample poll of citizen opinion, on discussions with community leaders, and on the prevalent dogma of metropolitan reform with its penchant for local federalism. These were slender reeds to depend on as future events were to demonstrate.

[8] Thomas H. Eliot, "Dilemmas in Metropolitan Research," *Midwest Journal of Political Science*, February 1958, p. 37. See also John C. Bollens, ed., *op. cit.*, where the rationale for the survey's decisions is discussed at length.

TWO

The Freeholders

The survey recommendations were released in late August 1957. Their reception was generally favorable. The two metropolitan dailies gave the report unusually extensive coverage and editorially lauded the proposals. Community leaders and civic organizations accepted the suggestions as a blueprint for action. Public officials were more cautious in their comments but few were openly critical. At this point, even the opponents of governmental reorganization considered it unwise to attack openly a study that had acquired so high a degree of respectability in the public mind.

The way was now open for action. Five days after the recommendations were made public, the Citizens Committee for City-County Co-ordination filed its petitions for the appointment of a metropolitan charter-drafting board. The committee's long period of self-abnegation had come to an end; the official machinery of reform had been set in motion.

The committee's frustrations, however, were not yet ended. In checking the county petitions, the election board invalidated all but 4,926 of the 13,430 signatures submitted, leaving the county petitions 2,834 short of the required number. What was perhaps a worse blow, the state's attorney general ruled that supplemental signatures could not be added to make up the shortage in the initial filing, indicating that the committee had to start anew the back-breaking task of collecting almost 8,000 signatures. Rejection of the county petitions raised a further legal question. The city petitions had been officially certified as sufficient, but the question now was whether the deficiencies in county signatures had not invalidated the whole procedure. If so, new signatures had also to be obtained in the city. The attorney general's opinion avoided this point, and

10

fortunately for the sponsors of the reform campaign, the implied threat to the validity of the city petitions never materialized although the question was widely discussed.

Disappointed but not overwhelmed by the setback, the citizens committee mustered its forces to assemble the new signatures. Six months of effort were required to accomplish this task, and in March 1958 petitions bearing almost 13,000 names were filed with the county election board. One month later the board announced that valid signatures in the amount required by law had been counted.

The next move belonged to the appointing authorities. The long delay in bringing a drafting commission into operation had dissipated much of the interest and enthusiasm displayed at the time the survey recommendations were made public. The petition fiasco had created an unfavorable public impression by casting doubt on the competence of those urging reorganization. It was in this milieu that the board of freeholders assumed its pivotal role.

THE BOARD IS APPOINTED

Under the Missouri Constitution a metropolitan charter-drafting commission, or board of freeholders, for the St. Louis area consists of 19 members, 9 from the city, an equal number from the county, and 1 from elsewhere in the state. The provisions for appointing such a board are unusual. City members are selected by the mayor and the city's 18 circuit court judges; those from the county by a group composed of the 7 county council members and the county's 9 circuit and probate court judges. The nineteenth member is designated by the governor, presumably for the purpose of preventing a deadlock between the city and county representatives.

The inadequacies of the method of appointment need only a little elucidation. One appointing group combines the mayor, a major political leader in the city, and 18 nonpartisan state judges. There would be some rationale for the arrangement if the city's chief executive could appoint 9 freeholders subject to confirmation by the circuit judges, but instead, the mayor's vote is only 1 of 19 cast for the city delegates. The selective procedure for county members is equally unusual. Neither the county supervisor, the counterpart of the central city mayor, nor members of the suburban municipal governments are included in the selection group. Instead, the entire county council together with the circuit and probate court judges, all elected on partisan ballots, constitute the appointing authority. This highly unorthodox method dilutes responsibility for the appointments and excludes the people from directly participating in the choice of delegates to the metropolitan constitutional assembly.

Since the two appointing groups transacted their business in executive sessions, little information is available as to how they reached their decisions. The minutes of the meetings released to the public include no list of the nominees considered. City representatives were chosen in October 1957 after petition signatures in that jurisdiction had been certified as sufficient. Names of the appointees, however, were withheld for six months until the county was ready to submit its list. On May 1, 1958, simultaneous announcements of the city and county appointments were made. One week later, the governor selected the nineteenth member.

THE FREEHOLDERS: THEIR QUALIFICATIONS

Formulating a plan of government for a metropolitan area of 1.5 million people is a time-consuming task that demands broad political skills. It is not an assignment for the inexperienced or small-minded nor an honorary post for the socially prominent—although men epitomizing these characteristics will always be found among constitution makers. Outstanding or poor boards are easy to recognize and identify. When, however, the personnel falls between these two extremes, assessment and categorization become more difficult. Such was the St. Louis case.

The county appointees included three businessmen, three lawyers, two union officials, and a university professor. Their total experience in public affairs was not impressive. Two of the businessmen, Charles F. Vatterott, a land developer and building contractor, and Adelbert Von Gontard, a director of Anheuser-Busch, had no previous experience in local government or politics. The third businessman, Vincent Bayer, was a part-time mayor of a small suburban village. The three lawyer members from the county had participated in various ways in local political life. H. M. Stolar had served as president of the St. Louis Board of Education before emigrating to the county; Bryan Purteet had been a board member of a suburban school district; and Eugene Buder, a recently defeated candidate for United States Congress, was active in Democratic party politics. One of the labor members, Dale Ferris, a business representative of the local teamsters union, had been chairman of the AFL-CIO Committee on Political Education; the other, Edwin Brown, was secretary-treasurer of the Electrical, Radio, and Machine Workers Union. He had no prior experience in public office. Mrs. Helen Graham, one of two women on the board, was a professor of pharmacology at Washington University and widow of the famed lung surgeon Dr. Evarts A. Graham. She had long been interested in county reorganization and had helped write the county civil service ordinance.

The pattern among the city members closely paralleled that of the county, although the public experience of its representatives was somewhat greater. The appointments included four businessmen, three lawyers, a union representative, and a housewife. All but one of the businessmen had served in various public capacities in St. Louis. Harry Simmons was a former chairman of the city civil service commission; Charles P. Orchard had been on the police board; and Ancel A. Skaggs was formerly chairman of the Republican central committee. Firmin Desloge, an industrialist and member of a prominent St. Louis family, had had no prior public service. Two of the lawyer members, James McClellan and Sidney Redmond, had been politically active. McClellan, in addition to his Republican party interests, had been chairman of a citizens tax committee appointed by city authorities. Redmond, the only Negro freeholder on the board, had served as an alderman. The third lawyer member, Richard Shewmaker, was a former president of the St. Louis Bar Association. Mrs. Rogers Deakin, the housewife, was active in the League of Women Voters and Republican ward politics. Russell Egan, the labor representative, was vice-president of the AFL-CIO St. Louis Labor Council and formerly business agent for the Municipal Firefighters' Union.

Veryl Riddle, the gubernatorial appointee, completed the list. A resident and city attorney of Malden, a small town located 175 miles south of St. Louis, Riddle was active in Democratic state politics. Because the nonlocal member, unlike the others, receives remuneration for his services, patronage considerations usually predominate in dictating his choice. With Riddle's selection the political alignment on the board was nine Democrats, eight Republicans, and two independents.

Restrained but polite approval greeted the announcement of the selections. The *Post-Dispatch* characterized the appointees as "fairly representative of metropolitan leadership," but then went on to comment: "Quite obviously some of the members do not come as highly recommended as others."[1] To those who believed that only strong leadership from the top ranks of the community power structure could bring metropolitan cooperation in the St. Louis area, the personnel of the board was a disappointment. No one disputed the statement of the local press that the appointees "were men and women of ideas and integrity," but some people saw the need for more than "ideas and integrity" on the part of the freeholders if the leadership and public education necessary to achieve metropolitan reorganization were to be forthcoming.

Most of the members were unknown to a wide public audience and few of them were recognized as community leaders. No one of major stature in local government and politics was included among the appointees; neither was the elite of the local business structure. The influential Civic Progress, Incorporated, and the top leadership of the chamber of commerce were not included. Key officials of civic organizations were also missing. Only the officialdom of the unions was well represented.

The composition of the board prompted some observers to conclude that city and county authorities had, through their appointments, guaranteed that the *status quo* would not be disturbed. This charge, however, lacks credence because it presupposes that the appointing groups pursued a conscious purpose in their

---

[1] May 5, 1958.

choice of board personnel. Actually, there are more indications that the contrary is true and that a haphazard selection process involving little or no unified direction was utilized in both city and county.

The principal problem faced by the appointing officials was not one of reconciling conflicting pressures but of finding 18 reasonably prominent persons who were willing to give the better part of a year to an arduous and complicated task. It is not surprising to find the names of the economically dominant and politically influential absent from the appointment list, perhaps because of time limitations in the first case and little political profit and many hazards in the latter. What *is* surprising in the St. Louis situation is the slight degree of concern displayed by major interest groups in the matter of appointments. Some organization spokesmen suggested names but others had to be solicited for recommendations.

Apparently the prolonged uncertainty over the filing of the petitions had dispelled any sense of urgency on the part of those who might have been concerned with the choice of freeholders. Apparently also the political leaders and others who might be affected by area-wide reorganization felt little need at this point to make their power felt. At any rate' there was no overt interest displayed over the appointments by any of the large pressure groups. From all available evidence, members of the two appointing authorities proposed names, some of which had been suggested to them by individuals and organizations; the nominations were then considered, with some attempt to secure balanced representation; and the final selections were made by majority vote.

ORGANIZING THE BOARD

Organizing a new commission, many members of which are strangers to each other, usually requires considerable sparring and negotiation before agreement is reached on officers and major procedures. In the St. Louis case, however, little maneuvering for position took place before the initial meeting of the board on May 19. Riddle, as the neutral representative from outside, was chosen temporary chairman without dissent. He in turn appointed a rules committee of six members from among volunteers for the assignment. Shewmaker, who was soon to prove one of the stronger members of the board, was named chairman.

The proposed rules presented by the committee ten days later were adopted with only minor amendments by the full board. The accepted rules provided for seven standing committees, two concerned with the housekeeping and public-relations functions of the board, the other five with the substantive features of a plan of government. The key committee of the latter group was that on the primary functions of government. This committee was charged with the important tasks of considering what governmental functions "should be vested in a metropolitan government" and what type of administrative or executive structure should be established for such an agency.[2]

On the same day the rules were adopted, the board also chose its permanent officers. The ease with which this was accomplished indicated that agreement on the selections had been reached prior to the meeting. The choice of the chairman, however, came as a surprise. Riddle, the temporary chairman whom many considered the logical choice for the office as a neutral participant, was overwhelmingly passed over in favor of Vatterott, the subdivision developer who by his own admission had little knowledge of metropolitan governmental affairs. The other officers were selected without opposition: Shewmaker as vice-chairman, Buder as secretary, and Egan as assistant secretary, thus balancing city and county representation.

Vatterott, who described himself as an "independent Republican," was not unknown in the St. Louis area although this was his first venture in the field of public service. His real estate, building construction, and banking activities were both prosperous and numerous, and he was prominent in Roman Catholic church affairs. The reasons for his unexpected choice as chairman of the charter-drafting board are not profound. At informal discussions between key city and county representatives on the board following the first meeting, agreement was reached that a county freeholder should be designated as chairman. Those participating in these negotiations purportedly felt that the most pressing problems calling for metropolitan reorganization were those of the county, and therefore any solution offered to the public should come under the chairmanship of a suburban representative. This also eliminated Riddle, because following this line of thinking, any plan developed with an "outsider" as chairman would be prejudicial in the public mind.

One might speculate in the light of later developments that more subtle reasoning lay behind the willingness of key city members to accept a county chairman. Presumably any proposal drafted under the leadership of such an individual would not be tainted as a "city plan" and consequently not automatically anathema to suburban residents. The likely strategy for the city members was to support the appointment of a county member as chairman and then attempt to coopt him into their cause. This line of speculation, while unverified, finds credence in the events that followed.

The choice of Vatterott from among the county representatives is an interesting example of the process of elimination. The informal preselection caucusing produced agreement that the chairman should be chosen from among those county members who would be the most "open-minded" on metropolitan reorganization and least likely to arouse the animosity of sizeable blocs of voters because of their prior activities or interest-group ties. Accordingly, Brown and Ferris were eliminated as labor representatives, Bayer as a local government

[2] Rules of Metropolitan Board of Freeholders, adopted May 28, 1958.

official, and Buder as a political activist. Purteet and Stolar, both able lawyers, were also excluded from consideration, the first because of his large corporate practice and his close association with leading county businessmen, the second because of his former position as head of the St. Louis City school board. With these eliminations the list was narrowed to three nonlawyer candidates: Mrs. Graham, Von Gontard, and Vatterott. Mrs. Graham was passed over because of the board's preference for a male as chairman, and Von Gontard removed himself from consideration by announcing that he was leaving for Europe on a business tour. The choice open to the freeholders was clear.

During the week following his selection as chairman, Vatterott conferred extensively with Shewmaker and others on committee assignments. The rules authorized him to appoint the standing committees with board approval. Vatterott's selections, which closely observed city-county and Democratic-Republican balances, were accepted by the board without dissent. The key appointment, that of head of the committee on primary functions of government, went to Shewmaker, with McClellan as cochairman. Shewmaker now occupied two important posts, an added reward no doubt for his role in the selection of the board chairman. As vice-chairman of the board and cochairman of its most important committee he was in a strategic position to influence the work of the freeholders.

With the employment of an office staff and legal counsel the organizational phase of the board was completed. Facing the freeholders was the monumental task of devising a workable plan for metropolitan reform, a plan that would be legally compatible with the state constitution and statutes and politically acceptable to separate majorities of voters in the city and county. The assignment, moreover, had to be completed within one year as prescribed by the constitution.

THREE

The Freeholders at Work

From the start of the board's deliberations, deep-seated differences among the members were apparent. Despite the usual declarations of open-mindedness, it soon became evident that some, perhaps even a majority, of the freeholders were strongly disposed toward either the merger or metropolitan-district approaches to constitutional reform. This split first manifested itself in the discussions over procedure. At least four members (Purteet, Graham, Buder, and Bayer) accepted most of the research findings of the survey. And while perhaps only the first two would at the outset have gone so far as to accept the recommendation of a multi-purpose district, all four seemed to believe that little purpose would be served by reexamining the same problems that the survey had documented. This group argued, therefore, that the board's deliberations and hearings should concentrate on the best means of solving these problems by governmental reform.

The second group, which was soon to show its distinct preference for total consolidation, insisted that the initial round of hearings should concentrate on ascertaining how citizens and public officials regarded the problems and needs of the metropolitan area. Those who early became identified with this faction included Shewmaker, Ferris, Egan, and Deakin. Their position on procedure prevailed, and at the fourth meeting of the board, Shewmaker's committee on primary functions of government was authorized to conduct a series of hearings on various problems including transportation, police, sanitation, land use, taxation, and education. Shewmaker, who was to emerge as the able and influential leader of the promerger faction, emphasized that his committee was not committed to the survey's district solution, or for that matter, to any of the other

17

three constitutional alternatives. The problems that his committee discovered would, he said, dictate the form of remedy.

STRATEGIES

The findings and recommendations of the survey became an issue within the board almost from the first meeting and remained a point of controversy through the final vote on the plan. Those, such as Purteet, who favored a limited approach to governmental reform, constantly sought to legitimize or support their position by referring to the survey's conclusions and the "experts" who conducted the study. Those who advocated a total solution, or political amalgamation, recognized the survey as an impediment to their objectives and concertedly endeavored to minimize its influence. Their strategy, largely shaped and executed by Shewmaker, took several forms.

First of all, the dissidents implied that the survey had recommended the district approach only because merger was regarded as politically unacceptable. Chairman Vatterott, who indicated his preference for consolidation early in the proceedings, said at one point when the survey was cited as authority against merger, "I've talked to many of the authors, several of the authors [sic], of the Metropolitan Survey and to other people close to the field of political science, and they believe that the one-area approach is the right thing, but they don't think it will be bought."[1] Shewmaker also kept insisting that the survey recommended a district because those who conducted the study "didn't think anything else would pass." When someone referred to results of the survey's attitude poll indicating strong opposition to merger, he retorted that we should ask "these political scientists whether they were recommending what they thought was best or whether they were engaged in conducting a popularity contest."

Secondly, those disposed toward merger endeavored to show that the district plan could not legally accomplish the objectives which the survey proposed. For example, one of the critical problems highlighted by the study was uncoordinated land-use planning. Yet, argued the consolidationists, a district government could not legally assume the function because the state constitution authorizes a metropolitan agency to take over "services" only, and land-use planning is not a service. Other legal obstacles, such as the bonding limitations on a district, were also cited at great length.

Finally, the freeholder critics of the study repeatedly emphasized that most functions of importance demand metropolitan handling and this fact was recognized by the writers of the survey when assigning the significant services to a

[1] This and the following quotations in this paragraph are from the transcript of the Meeting of the Committee of the Whole, Metropolitan Board of Freeholders, October 30, 1958.

district government. Hence, the single-government proponents insisted, because effective reorganization in any form requires that the important functions be taken away from the municipalities, the freeholders might as well create an efficient and economical unit rather than add another agency to an already cumbersome system. "You can call the district what you like," Shewmaker observed, "but it's still putting powers in one central body." If the people, in other words, will not accept merger they will not accept a multipurpose district.

The prodistrict freeholders, led by Purteet, attempted to counter the strategy of the Shewmaker faction by demonstrating through testimony at the public hearings that many influential community leaders and groups were opposed to merger on grounds other than expediency. In answer to the legal questions raised by the mergerites, Purteet and his group sought to show that political consolidation would involve many more legal difficulties than the district plan because the district approach had already been tested in the courts in connection with the metropolitan sewer district. As against the argument that the district would take away the significant powers of the municipalities, supporters stressed the limited character of their approach and the many important powers that would remain with the local units.

These issues assumed importance from the beginning because of the rapid formation of the two opposing sides within the board. Leaders of each bloc early recognized that the balance of power rested in the hands of the uncommitted freeholders and that the outcome depended on the direction taken by these members. The arguments, however, were also aimed beyond the freeholders to the general public. A large number of the board's meetings were televised on KETC, the educational channel in St. Louis, and these broadcasts provided each faction with additional opportunities to muster outside support for its position.

COMMITTEE HEARINGS ON PROBLEMS

Hearings by the committee on primary functions of government began in June and continued until August 1958. Numerous invitations were sent to governmental officials, civic organizations, interest groups, and community leaders. The committee patiently sat through long hours of testimony, much of it only of peripheral concern to the major task. The hopes of the promergerites that these sessions would provide effective ammunition for their cause began to dwindle as the hearings dragged on through the hot summer months. If anything, the testimony served to vindicate the findings of the survey as to the needs and problems of the area.

Spokesmen who appeared before the committee generally agreed on the need for some type of area-wide authority in such matters as traffic, planning, economic development, and civil defense. On most other services, however, reactions to major changes were negative. The consensus, as the committee was forced to conclude in its reports to the board, was that no need existed for consolidation of such services as police and fire protection, sanitation, health, hospitals, and garbage disposal.

As the pattern of the hearings was repeated over and over again, some of the freeholders began to exhibit signs of impatience with the procedure. The first move to shift the emphasis from ascertaining public views to substantive action on a plan came at the thirteenth meeting of the board early in August when Purteet formally presented his district proposal. His move precipitated the introduction of four additional plans by other members during the course of the next six weeks. It also halted the procedure that was being followed and led to a decision to suspend further public hearings until the board tentatively decided on the plan or proposal that would be submitted to the voters.

THE REORGANIZATION PROPOSALS

When Purteet submitted his draft plan, he stated that his purpose was to give the group an outline as a basis for its considerations which, he felt, had lacked a unified purpose to this point. His proposal, modeled on the recommendations of the survey but more extensive in scope, called for the creation of a multipurpose district authority to administer certain area-wide services. In introducing his plan, Purteet emphasized that it was only a check list of possible powers that might be granted to a district government. Later he introduced a second version of his plan that brought the powers of the district government closely in line with those suggested by the survey.

Three weeks after Purteet's move, Freeholder Stolar introduced a second proposal for the board's consideration to the effect that the city of St. Louis reenter St. Louis County under the second constitutional alternative. As a corollary to his plan, Stolar called on the board to recommend enlargement by constitutional amendment of the county's power to provide area-wide services. In this way, he argued, all the advantages of the district plan could be secured and its disadvantages avoided. Some observers believed that Stolar, who was known to be on friendly terms with Mayor Tucker, introduced his proposal at the latter's request. It was common knowledge for several weeks prior to Stolar's action that the mayor had come to favor this approach among those available under the constitution. One week after the plan was submitted, Tucker stated in a television interview that although reentry did not go to the root of the area's problems, it was more acceptable to the city than any other proposal. The main advantage, he stated, was its simplicity, because it utilized the existing county government as the area-wide authority.

On September 18, a third proposal was presented by Buder. His plan called for utilization of two of the four constitutional alternatives. The city would reenter the county, as proposed by Stolar, and the existing county government would be designated as a multipurpose district under the fourth constitutional power. Buder argued that his approach would retain all the advantages of Purteet's district plan and Stolar's reentry proposal without creating a new "layer of government" as the first suggestion would or requiring a constitutional amendment as the second would before the county government could become the metropolitan vehicle.

Shortly after Buder offered his plan, the two final proposals were simultaneously presented to the board under the joint sponsorship of Shewmaker, McClellan, and Vatterott. The first of these provided for a limited multipurpose district; the second utilized the merger alternative in the constitution to propose a single government for the metropolitan area to be known as the "municipal county." The district plan included six substantive functions: traffic control, operation of public transit, land-use planning, civil defense, assessment, and sewage disposal. Unlike the Purteet draft which provided for a new governing board, the joint proposal utilized existing city and county officers as a legislative commission for the district. The "municipal county" plan, on the other hand, provided for the consolidation of all existing local governments in the area with the exception of the school districts.

The introduction of two such drastically different solutions by the same group apparently came at McClellan's insistence. It was well known by this time that Shewmaker was strongly in favor of merger and opposed to any lesser approach. He and McClellan were long-time friends and the two of them had planned to submit a joint proposal from the beginning of the board's existence. McClellan also leaned toward merger but at the same time he felt that the freeholders should have a clear choice before them between a moderate proposal utilizing existing governmental institutions and a plan that was total in effect. As he stated at the time the plans were introduced:

> We are aware, of course, that there are those who feel this proposal [municipal county] goes too far and that this board should instead adopt a plan providing for the establishment of a district government to handle certain essential services common to the whole metropolitan area. While we do not share this opinion, we recognize that the board must necessarily give full and careful consideration to this method. Accordingly, we have submitted proposal number 4, which provides for a simplified district authority.[2]

To what extent this also may have been a calculated attempt to detract attention from Purteet's plan and prevent the uncommitted from casting their lot with him could not be ascertained.

Because Shewmaker and McClellan were both city residents, Vatterott was

2 *Ibid.*

brought into the early discussions of the proposal. Still later, Ferris, also a county resident, was consulted in order to broaden the plan's sponsorship. Ferris then undertook to win the support of top union leaders for the proposal. The union men indicated that they were favorable to consolidation as a general solution to the area's problems, but they refused to back publicly the "municipal county" plan at the time. While leaving the door open for future endorsement, they expressed several reservations about the proposal, one of which related to the extension of the city's nonpartisan court plan to the county, where judges are elected on partisan ballots. (Labor's opposition to nonpartisan elections was repeatedly stressed by labor representatives on the board.) As a result of the labor leaders' refusal to endorse the merger proposal, Ferris withdrew as a sponsor before the plan was introduced.

SPONSORSHIP OF THE PROPOSALS

The sponsorship of the five plans can be explained only partially. Purteet's introduction of the district proposal is easiest to understand. He was closely associated both socially and professionally with many of the key leaders in the county chamber of commerce. This group generally favored moderate reorganization but vigorously opposed political consolidation. Purteet saw in the survey recommendations a moderate route to metropolitan reform and hence became an ardent advocate of such proposals.

The impetus for Stolar's reentry plan has already been noted. Buder's combined reentry-district proposal was an attempt by a young and independently minded lawyer to find legal means of utilizing existing governmental machinery. A county resident and a proponent of local federalism, Buder was convinced that merger was wholly unrealistic. He was impressed by the research and findings of the survey but he sensed the political effectiveness of the argument against creating another level of government. When asked at the time whether he would favor reentry if it could not be combined legally with the district, he replied, "No, I would definitely favor power 4 [district] in that case." [3]

Sponsorship of the merger plan is the most difficult to explain. As city residents, Shewmaker and McClellan might reasonably have been expected to favor consolidation as the desirable remedy. What is puzzling, however, is the intransigent attitude of the former throughout the proceedings, his unwillingness to compromise, and his refusal to sign the district plan ultimately adopted by the board. Shewmaker was a partner in a prominent law firm that numbered many of the area's major business interests among its clientele. He was not particularly active in politics or close to labor. His unyielding stand can be explained only on

[3] Transcript of Meeting of the Committee of the Whole, Metropolitan Board of Freeholders, October 16, 1958.

personal grounds. A man of strong convictions, he looked upon merger as the most desirable remedy; he was determined to sustain his viewpoint.

McClellan, who was active in Republican city politics, was more flexible in his attitude. As Shewmaker's position became more adamant in the face of growing opposition in the board, McClellan's desire to forestall a disastrous deadlock led him on occasion to vote with the moderates. Also unlike his colleague, McClellan signed the district plan after it prevailed on the final vote.

How Vatterott, a county resident and suburban businessman, was brought into the sponsoring triumvirate is equally puzzling. He obviously approached his task with an open mind and a sincere desire to find a suitable remedy for the area's problems. In his efforts to learn about the needs of metropolitan reorganization, he went so far as to employ a research assistant at his own expense. He also sought the advice of knowledgeable individuals both within and outside the board. One of those he listened to was the Reverend Edward Dowling, a Jesuit who had long been active in civic reform movements and who was a staunch supporter of city-county merger. Vatterott early began to turn to freeholders McClellan, Ferris, and Shewmaker. These three members, later to prove the core of the merger bloc, were highly recommended to Vatterott by his personal confidants, such as Father Dowling, on whom he relied heavily in evaluating the individual freeholders. The three soon came to exercise a noticeable influence in shaping Vatterott's attitude toward metropolitan reform.

Vatterott, however, was never certain of the full implications of merger. As time went on, he began to sense the deep resistance of county residents to the loss of their local autonomy. Disturbed by this awareness, he later insisted that the merger plan provide for the retention of certain governmental powers at the local level. Many of his modifications were embodied in the merger proposal but their inclusion did little to mitigate the effects of total consolidation. Under the constitutional alternatives open to the freeholders, merger and local autonomy were mutually incompatible concepts. The acceptance of the first in any form meant the destruction of the latter.

SELECTING THE PLAN

In the months following introduction of the five plans, long debates over their respective merits and deficiencies took place among the board members. Some of the discussions touched upon fundamental political and administrative principles but the majority of the sessions bogged down in legal intricacies. The seven lawyer freeholders then dominated the discussions while the other members could only say with Mrs. Graham, after an evening of legal sparring, "My mind is full of legal ifs and buts."

By late 1958, it was evident that the choice lay between two plans: Purteet's district proposal and the merger. Stolar's reentry scheme, although it was to be revived during the last of the board meetings had attracted little support because few freeholders wanted to rely on the subsequent passage of a constitutional amendment. They were informed by counsel, moreover, that reentry of the city into the county would bar future use of the constitutional alternatives. Buder's plan interested many of the members, but serious doubts that the two alternatives could be legally combined discouraged support for it. The simplified district proposal of McClellan, Shewmaker, and Vatterott was never developed or pushed by its sponsors after its submission.

Starting in November, a series of maneuvers took place within the board that revealed the close division among the members and left the outcome in doubt until the final vote. The first move came on a successful motion to have the appropriate committees concentrate on preparing two plans: merger and district. Merger proponents followed up this action by introducing a resolution at the December 18 meeting to proceed with the development of the merger plan only. On this test of strength the motion carried by a vote of 10 to 8 with Orchard (who had suffered a heart attack) absent. Less than one month later, Simmons, who had voted with the majority in limiting consideration to the merger proposal, moved to rescind the December 18 action and reinstate the earlier resolution calling for the preparation of two plans. After a motion to table was defeated by a vote of 11 to 7, Simmons' motion carried 14 to 4 with Mrs. Deakin and the three union representatives in opposition. Each of the two plans was then assigned to a special committee composed of five adherents. On the municipal county, or merger, committee were McClellan as chairman, Deakin, Egan, Ferris, and Shewmaker. The district committee was composed of Purteet as chairman, Graham, Bayer, Buder, and Redmond.

Simmons' apparent defection from the ranks of the consolidationists placed their cause in jeopardy. Not only his own support but that of Orchard's was now at stake. The two were close friends and it was generally anticipated that Orchard, who attended infrequently because of ill health, would follow the lead of Simmons.

On April 2, as the time for final decision drew near, Stolar, in a surprise maneuver, again proposed that the reentry alternative be developed along with the merger and district plans. The motion lost by a tie vote of 8 to 8. Merger proponents who up to this time had shown little interest in the Stolar proposal now voted solidly for the motion. Conversely, the district faction that had evidenced some sympathy with this approach in the past unanimously opposed the motion. The promergerites, in an effort to head off victory by the district proponents, had apparently persuaded Stolar to reintroduce his proposal at this late date with assurances of their support. At this stage, however, the time for possible compromise had passed.

Two weeks later, on April 15, the final count was taken. The district plan had squeezed through by the narrow margin of 10 votes to 9. Supporting each plan were the following freeholders:

Multipurpose district	Municipal county (merger)
Bayer	Brown
Buder	Deakin
Desloge	Egan
Graham	Ferris
Orchard	McClellan
Purteet	Riddle
Redmond	Shewmaker
Simmons	Skaggs
Stolar	Vatterott
Von Gontard	

Five members of the consolidation faction, Shewmaker, Mrs. Deakin, and the three union representatives, refused to sign the final plan and it went to the voters without their blessing.

POLITICAL BEHAVIOR OF FREEHOLDERS

The fact that many officials were involved in the selection of the freeholders leads to the expectation of a diversely constituted commission lacking in any previously established pattern of interrelationships. This assumption in turn suggests that the board's deliberations would be characterized by a high degree of instability and disorganization manifested by many similar groupings among the freeholders. However, the rapid appearance of a few sharply distinct factions within the board casts doubt on these assumptions and prompts more careful examination of group behavior among the members.

To assist in analyzing the political behavior of the board, the nonunanimous roll-call votes through its year of deliberations were subjected to conventional bloc analysis.[4] For this purpose, the hypothesis was advanced that "the final vote by the freeholders on the plan to be presented to the people revealed alignments, the members of which had in fact voted as highly cohesive blocs throughout the board's existence." The analysis supports generally this assumption. A high degree of polarization of the freeholders into two cohesive voting blocs is shown, each bloc supporting with strong solidarity one of the two major proposals: merger or metropolitan district. A third pivotal group also is identified, revealing that the shifts in position of members of the third group eventually determined the board's final decision.

The matrix in Table 1 represents the percentage of paired agreements over

[4] See Appendix for a description of the methodology employed.

TABLE 1

Paired Agreements among Freeholders on 36 Nonunanimous Roll Call Votes

(Expressed in Percentages)

	Bayer	Graham	Desloge	Von Gontard	Purteet	Buder	Stolar	Simmons	Redmond	Skaggs	Egan	Brown	Ferris	Deakin	Shewmaker	McClellan	Riddle	Vatterott
Bayer		82	76	76	77	61	73	70	77	62								
Graham			74	86	79	75	63	75	68	61								
Desloge				79	81	74	65	63	65							63		
Von Gontard					95	82	71	77		67						76		
Purteet						79	74	61		61						60		
Buder							70			61						77		66
Stolar									68	70								
Simmons										64							68	
Redmond																		
Skaggs																		71
Egan												91	87	88	80	73	73	75
Brown													92	88	80	73	75	79
Ferris														85	84	83	83	88
Deakin															79	77	88	83
Shewmaker																87	87	91
McClellan																	95	97
Riddle																		100
Vatterott																		

(Annotations on the table: a box enclosing the upper-left group is labeled "Merger bloc"; a box enclosing the lower-right group is labeled "District bloc".)

Index of cohesion for District bloc 0.758; Merger bloc 0.843

possible agreements among 18 freeholders in 36 nonunanimous roll-call votes.[5] Percentages of agreed pairs under 60 percent have been arbitrarily excluded for more graphic presentation of the bloc alignments. Thus, in identifying cohesive voting factions, 60 percent of paired agreements with all other members of a bloc is the criterion for inclusion in the group. When this procedure is employed, two highly cohesive blocs immediately become evident in the matrix. The bloc in the upper-left quadrant comprises 7 members who supported the district plan on the final vote; that in the lower-right quadrant includes 8 who voted for the merger proposal on the final tally.

Several pertinent observations can be drawn from this general matrix. First, the merger bloc was not only slightly larger (8 members) than the district faction (7 members) but it was also considerably more cohesive. Using the mean of the percentages included within the bloc as a simple measure, the index of cohesion for the merger group is 0.843 compared to 0.758 for the district bloc. This high degree of unity enabled the consolidationists to come within a single vote of securing adoption of the municipal-county plan despite widespread doubts of its feasibility among a majority of board members.

Second, two highly cohesive subblocs appear among the mergerites. The first is that of labor—Egan, Brown, and Ferris—who show a cohesion rate of 0.900 through the 36 votes. The second consists of McClellan, Riddle, and Vatterott who, although they did not act consciously as a group, had an almost perfect index of 0.973. Their deviation from other members of the bloc occurred almost exclusively on motions that would leave the door open to other approaches, particularly reentry. Shewmaker, the acknowledged leader of the mergerites, had a lower cohesion rate with these three members, indicating that he pushed his demands too far at times. Among the district adherents, only Purteet and Von Gontard show paired agreements of over 80 percent, further corroborating the greater degree of fluidity in this group.

Third, in addition to the two polar blocs, the matrix reveals a pivotal subgroup composed of three freeholders—Redmond, Skaggs, and Simmons. These three could not properly be designated a bloc since they did not act in concert and their cohesion rate was low. Redmond, the only Negro on the board, was obviously from the start an antimergerite although not necessarily a prodistrict adherent. His lack of sympathy for merger is evidenced by the fact that he had no paired agreements of over 60 percent with any member of the consolidation bloc. Skaggs was the most ambivalent of the three, recording paired agreements of over 60 percent with five members of each of the two major divisions.

Simmons appears from the table to lean strongly toward the district bloc, yet

---

[5] A total of 44 nonunanimous votes were taken during the course of the board's existence but 8 were decided without roll-call vote and the divisions therefore were not recorded. Freeholder Orchard is omitted from the tabulation because his illness allowed him to participate in only 6 of the 36 roll-call votes.

his key pivotal role (enhanced by his influence on the vote of the incapacitated Orchard) is more clearly revealed when two refinements of the general matrix are made. Although omitted here because of space limitations, matrices were prepared showing the number of paired agreements of freeholders when voting in the minority and when roll calls in which majorities in each bloc voted together were eliminated from consideration.[6] In each case the over-all alignment is similar to that in Table 1. Redmond, however, appears in the district bloc with Skaggs again in an ambivalent position and Simmons is definitely outside both clusters. Stolar and Buder who are well within the prodistrict group in the general and minority vote matrices narrowly fall outside when bi-bloc votes are removed from the computation. Buder and Stolar, it will be recalled, submitted separate proposals, and while they frequently expressed their commitment to a limited solution, they at times voted against the district bloc in the interests of preserving their own plans.

To investigate more carefully the chronological switches in the voting pattern of the members, two additional matrices were constructed: one covering the period to the end of 1958 when Simmons appeared to change his stand, the other encompassing the remainder of the board's existence. (See Tables 2 and 3). Comparison of the two tables shows Simmons well within the merger quadrant for the first 17 votes, with a dramatic switch to the district alignment during the last 19 votes. The tables also reveal that both blocs were larger and more cohesive during the earlier period.

Obviously some of the freeholders began to feel less certain of the proper path to take as the deliberations turned to specific proposals and as numerous and involved legal questions were raised about each plan. The problem of the school system is one of many such examples. The consolidationists had provided in their proposal that the school districts remain unchanged. Yet the board's counsel advised that adoption of the merger plan would legally result in the creation of a single school district for the area. Although Shewmaker tried to shrug off this possibility, the freeholders realized the intense opposition that would be aroused among county residents to any plan involving abolition of their local school districts.

BLOC ALLEGIANCES

The important question that remains is the extent to which interest group or other allegiances contributed to the bloc formations and the high degree of cohesion within them. Two obvious categories for examination in this respect are the political affiliations of the freeholders and their places of residence. When the two blocs, minus the fringe members, are checked for these characteristics, the results shown in Table 4 are obtained.

[6] These two approaches are further described in the Appendix.

TABLE 2

PAIRED AGREEMENTS AMONG FREEHOLDERS ON 17 NONUNANIMOUS ROLL CALL VOTES THROUGH DECEMBER 1958
(EXPRESSED IN PERCENTAGES)

	Bayer	Purteet	Stolar	Von Gontard	Graham	Buder	Desloge	Redmond	Skaggs	Simmons	Egan	Brown	Ferris	Deakin	Shewmaker	McClellan	Vatterott	Riddle
Bayer		86	92	89	81	81	77	73	60									
Purteet			92	86	80	80	79	62										
Stolar				100	83	83	83		67									
Von Gontard					100	89	67		75	78						71	63	63
Graham						88	71	67	63									
Buder							86		60									
Desloge								67										
Redmond									60									
Skaggs										75			67	69	64	79	81	79
Simmons											69	67	73	76	87	87	88	87
Egan												100	100	92	85	83		85
Brown													100	83	83		82	82
Ferris														87	85	85	87	92
Deakin															87	87	88	92
Shewmaker																87	86	85
McClellan																	100	100
Vatterott																		100
Riddle																		

District bloc (enclosing Bayer through Desloge)

Merger bloc (enclosing Simmons through Riddle)

Index of cohesion for District bloc 0.844; Merger bloc 0.868

TABLE 3

PAIRED AGREEMENTS AMONG FREEHOLDERS ON 19 NONUNANIMOUS ROLL CALL VOTES JANUARY THROUGH APRIL 1959
(EXPRESSED IN PERCENTAGES)

	Pureet	Graham	Von Gontard	Simmons	Bayer	Desloge	Redmond	Buder	Stolar	Skaggs	McClellan	Riddle	Ferris	Egan	Brown	Deakin	Vatterott	Shewmaker
Pureet		77	100	77	67	85		77			80							
Graham			77	95	82	77	69	63			63							
Von Gontard				77	67	85		77			80							
Simmons					88	77	75				60							
Bayer						75	81			64								
Desloge							64	62			60							
Redmond									64	60								
Buder									60		88						68	63
Stolar										75								60
Skaggs											66							66
McClellan												86	75		60	69		88
Riddle													70		67	80	100	90
Ferris														75	85	84	89	84
Egan															82	83	66	90
Brown																92	77	77
Deakin																	79	74
Vatterott																		95
Shewmaker																		

District bloc (Pureet, Graham, Von Gontard, Simmons, Bayer, Desloge)

Merger bloc (Ferris, Egan, Brown, Deakin, Vatterott, Shewmaker)

Index of cohesion for District bloc 0.804; Merger bloc 0.821

TABLE 4

PARTY AFFILIATION AND PLACE OF RESIDENCE OF BLOC MEMBERS

| | District bloc | | | Merger bloc | |
Name	Party	Residence	Name	Party	Residence
Bayer	Dem.	Co.	Brown	Dem.	Co.
Buder	Dem.	Co.	Deakin	Rep.	City
Desloge	Ind.	City	Egan	Dem.	City
Graham	Ind.	Co.	Ferris	Dem.	Co.
Purteet	Rep.	Co.	McClellan	Rep.	City
Stolar	Rep.	Co.	Riddle	Dem.	Outstate
Von Gontard	Rep.	Co.	Shewmaker	Dem.	City
			Vatterott	Rep.	Co.

As the table shows, all but one of the district bloc are county residents. The single exception is Desloge, who had no party ties or previous public experience and who initially had no strong feelings toward any particular solution. It would not be surprising, then, were he to gravitate toward his social and business peers, Von Gontard and Purteet. The paired voting analysis supports this assumption because it shows that his cohesion index was highest with these two individuals. Ultimately the district bloc was joined by three other city residents: Redmond, a Republican, and Simmons and Orchard, Democrats. As a Negro, Redmond might have reflected the fears of politically active members of his race that merger would dilute their growing power in the core city by adding the overwhelmingly white suburbs to the electoral unit. The defection of Simmons, and thus of Orchard, from the city ranks requires further explanation.

To understand Simmons' defection, it is necessary to go back earlier than January 1959, when he began voting with the district bloc. His original position with the merger-minded freeholders can certainly be characterized as an uneasy alliance (see Table 2). As personnel director for a large local concern, Simmons was not regarded as friendly to labor. Yet in the merger bloc, the most deliberately cohesive subgroup was that comprising the three labor representatives. Even during the period when Simmons was within the merger bloc, his cohesion rate was the lowest of the 9-man group—0.793 as compared with a mean of 0.878 for the other 8 members.

Simmons' identification with the merger bloc began to weaken as certain developments took place. He considered the legal opinion that consolidation would destroy the autonomy of the county school systems a serious blow to the chances of the merger plan. At subsequent meetings of the board he joined with other nonlawyer members in objecting to Shewmaker's attempts to explain away the school issue in clouds of legal verbiage. Further, as acting chairman of the budget committee during Orchard's absence, he began to resent what he viewed as the merger bloc's high-handed disregard for the committee's prerogatives. This situation reached a climax in late December 1958, when he clashed unsuccessfully with the mergerites over the employment of Public Administration Service of Chicago to develop details of the merger plan. He had hoped to see the Governmental Research Institute of St. Louis rather than an outside firm assigned this responsibility. It was only six days after this dispute that he announced his intention to move the revival of the district plan's consideration. From this point forward, Simmons (and subsequently Orchard) voted consistently with the district bloc.

The geographical composition of the merger bloc was more heterogeneous than that of the district faction with three of the eight mergerites residing in the county and one outside the area. Two of the county appointees in this group, however, were union representatives, a fact which helps to explain their position. Labor, with its close ties to the city Democratic organization, generally indicated its preference for merger because it saw in such a solution the possibility of greater access to the metropolitan governmental machinery. Riddle, the outstate member and an active Democrat, could be expected to support whatever position was taken by the city Democrats and labor. Vatterott's deviation from the city-county alignment was more a matter of personal choice than any underlying force.

Political affiliation appears at most to be a secondary factor in contributing to the high degree of cohesiveness in the two blocs. The district group contained two Democrats, three Republicans, and two Independents; while the merger faction with five Democrats and three Republicans showed a somewhat more pronounced political pattern. Here city Democrats were joined by labor Democrats from the county and the outstate member. This faction also captured the support of the organizational Republicans in the city: Mrs. Deakin, McClellan, and ultimately Skaggs. City Democrats would profit from consolidation by extending their influence into the county; city Republicans, now hopelessly outnumbered, could only gain by such a change. Significantly, no county Republican other than Vatterott crossed over into this group.

The bloc analysis clearly substantiates the hypothesis that the final vote on the plans revealed cohesive alignments which had existed throughout most of the board's existence. It also verifies the assumption that place of residence was the most important variable in determining the factional affiliations. Only the labor representatives transcended this factor, and here functional interests molded them into a highly cohesive subbloc. The other deviations from the geographical pattern occurred for individual reasons as already noted. Political affiliations had some part in shaping the blocs but the method of appointing the freeholders and the separate party structures of the city and county largely neutralized the possible influence of party allegiances.

The paired voting analysis also substantiates the impression of close observers that the board conducted its deliberations free from outside pressures. Even the labor representatives, while reflecting the biases of their organizational affiliations, were left free to formulate their own policy. Careful probing and interviewing failed to reveal any evidence of covert attempts to influence the board. The major interest groups followed a "hands off" policy, showing little concern over the board's activities. Apparently they felt that little would come of the freeholders' work, and that if necessary they could always exercise an effective veto at the referendum stage.

FOUR

The Campaign for
Metropolitan Government

Almost three years of intensive study and deliberation had elapsed since
the institution of the survey in 1956. Six months now remained before the
voters of the city and county would be called upon to signify their acceptance
or rejection of the freeholders' work. The metropolitan constituent assembly
with the deep cleavage among its members had left a legacy of uncertainty to
the people and had failed to provide them with a common rallying point or a
center of leadership. The issues that were to dominate the ensuing campaign
had already taken shape in its deliberations. Reflected also in the position and
attitudes of the freeholders were the likely sources of support and opposition
to the plan.

The proposed charter was necessarily complex, lengthy, and detailed. How
could its contents, its meaning, and its intended purposes be communicated to
a large electorate and the uncertainty generated by the drafters dispelled within
this relatively short period of time? And how and by what means could the
area's leadership be effectively mobilized for the ensuing civic campaign?
These were troublesome questions that faced the proponents of metropolitan
reorganization as the time of public decision approached.

ORGANIZING FOR ACTION

All possible avenues for organizing the campaign were considered, including the use of the Board of Freeholders and the Citizens Committee for City-County Coordination. The first was eliminated because of the split in its membership which persisted even after the charter was presented for public consideration. The second group appeared the most logical agency for spearheading the campaign. It had been instrumental in creating the Board of Freeholders and had demonstrated its ability for organizing a large-scale movement in the face of discouraging setbacks. As already indicated, however, the committee was politically suspect and lacking in influential community members. Leaders of the group, moreover, were by this time less than enthusiastic about the plan; several of them, in fact, had become convinced that merger was the proper solution.

Despite these reservations among some of its members, the citizens committee had invested too much effort, time, and hard work in the reorganization movement to see it collapse for lack of leadership. When no other group appeared willing to expend the time and resources necessary to organize the campaign, the committee stepped into the void. As one of its officials stated, "We were not 100 percent sold on the district plan, but experts recommend it, and someone had to carry the ball. When no one else stepped up to do it, we figured it was our responsibility."

Civic and business leaders who had previously remained aloof from the committee now seemed willing to accept it as the campaign vehicle. The only alternative was to organize and conduct the campaign themselves, and this they were unwilling to do.

In order to broaden the base of support and remove the taint that had continually plagued it, the citizens committee was formally dissolved and a new organization known as the City-County Partnership Committee was formed. The first meeting on May 22, 1959 was attended by some 75 persons representing a wide variety of governmental, civic, and business interests. Over 400 invitations had been issued but only a minority of the invited groups sent representatives. Among the community leadership missing were the mayor of St. Louis, the county supervisor, and the political party chieftains. One official of the St. Louis Labor Council attended but remained silent.

At the time of the meeting the mayor had taken no public position on the plan, principally on the ground that he was actively engaged in a campaign to increase the city's earnings tax. The county supervisor had also refrained from any clear-cut stand, merely suggesting the need for more study. The Labor Council, whose president had been prominent in the earlier activities of the citizens committee, had indicated during the freeholders' sessions that it regarded merger of city and county as the most desirable remedy. At this time, the council had given no indication of its position on the district plan. The central committees of both political parties had likewise remained uncommitted.

Cervantes, the mainspring of the reorganization movement, presided at the meeting. The few speakers who expressed themselves agreed politely that the proposed plan had been carefully researched, that it was sound and practical, and that in any case the voters were now limited to a choice between the metropolitan district and continuance of the status quo. The group quickly agreed on the formal purpose of the new committee: "To promote the general welfare and orderly development and prosperity of St. Louis City and County by presenting to the people of this community for their favorable consideration the Greater St. Louis City-County District Plan."

Following this simple ritual, the chairman appointed an executive committee of fifteen members to formulate more specific plans for the campaign organization. In addition to Cervantes and his colleague on the old citizens committee, H. Jackson Daniel, the list included Edwin M. Clark, president of Southwestern Bell Telephone Company and a leading citizen; the presidents of the city and county chambers of commerce; the mayor of the largest suburban municipality who was currently serving as president of the County League of Municipalities; the former president of the League of Women Voters; and two members of the Board of Freeholders, Purteet, who had played a leading role in the development of the district plan, and Redmond, who had supported it. Missing from this array were the political and labor leaders of both city and county, those with the means and knowhow to mobilize the voters.

In the three months following its organizational meeting, the new committee evidenced few signs of life. St. Louis summers are hot and not conducive to active campaigning, but even the group's efforts to organize lagged. It was not until the end of August that campaign chairmen were announced. The general chairmanship went to William F. James, an automobile-firm executive and minor civic leader. James was best known for his work in connection with Boys Town of Missouri. His acceptance of the post was, by his own admission, his first venture into such matters as "politics and elections." He described himself as a "Republicrat," with no partisan leanings. James was surprised when the committee first approached him. As he stated, he had no knowledge of what the district plan "was all about"; but he took five days to study and discuss it with proponents and opponents. His decision to accept the appointment followed. "I was firmly convinced that here is what St. Louis needs because it is a step forward. . . . I felt it would be good for the County, which is where I live. I felt it would be good for my children."[1] These were noble sentiments but they gave no indication of capacity to assume the general direction of a major campaign.

[1] *St. Louis Globe-Democrat*, August 28, 1959.

The selection of James was as surprising to others as it was to himself. It was generally expected that some prominent civic leader would be given this assignment, but no one among the community elite could be persuaded to accept such an arduous role. By default, therefore, the appointment went to one in the lower ranks of leadership. City and county campaign chairmen were also named to complete the campaign organization: Cervantes in the city and Carroll J. Donohue in the county. The latter was a well-known attorney and former president of the local bar association. A Democrat, and a law partner of H. Jackson Daniel, he was active in county politics. Upon these three individuals fell the primary responsibility for arousing interest in a cause that up to this time had evoked little public response.

FORMATION OF THE OPPOSITION

While proponents of metropolitan reform were preparing for action, organized opposition made its appearance in the form of three different groups: the Webster Groves Task Force for Self-government, the Citizens Committee for Self-government, and the Citizens Committee against the District Plan. The first originated in suburban Webster Groves, a high-income community of long standing. The least important of the three opposition organizations, it was led by Vernon Riehl, a former Republican alderman in St. Louis City who had moved to Webster Groves some years earlier and had found there "the ideal place to live." This largely Republican group remained local throughout the campaign.

The second organization, the Citizens Committee for Self-government, constituted a more important source of opposition. Almost entirely county based, it was heavily weighted with Republican party leaders and municipal officials. Its president was the mayor of a large suburban community; one of its two vice-presidents was an extremely vocal businessman who claimed credit for defeating a recent attempt to consolidate three upper-income municipalities in the county; the other was editor of a suburban weekly. In addition to those with vested interests in retaining the existing governmental pattern, such as the Republican party stalwarts and local officeholders and employees, the organization attracted an agglomeration of chronic opposition groups including opponents of public housing, fluoridation, and federal income taxes.

The third opposing organization, the Citizens Committee against the District Plan, was created less than a month before the election. Bringing together the intransigent promergerites, the new group announced as its objectives: "To seek defeat of the Metropolitan District Plan because it does not go far enough"; and "to keep the way open for consolidation of City-County governments." Leaders of the organization stated that "it is not a question of the district or nothing. The question is rather whether the people of Greater St. Louis will have the vision to reject the timid and tragically inadequate district proposal in order to achieve the right solution to the real problem of government in our growing city-county community ... a single, unified great city."[2]

The leadership of this third group was impressive. Of its three cochairmen, one was the Democratic National Committeeman from Missouri; another, the Republican gubernatorial candidate in 1956 and a member of a prominent St. Louis family; and the third, president of the St. Louis AFL–CIO Labor Council. The spark plug behind the organization was Lemoine Skinner, a public relations consultant, among whose clients were the Vatterott interests. Skinner, who had long been an advocate of complete consolidation, had little difficulty in convincing the three cochairmen that creation of a metropolitan district would delay if not destroy the chances for total merger. This group, in contrast to the Citizens Committee for Self-government, drew its support almost entirely from city residents. And in marked contrast also, its grounds for opposition were exactly the reverse of those of the county organization.

THE LINE-UP FOR

As the campaign slowly progressed, efforts were made by both camps to enlist the various civic and interest groups and individual citizens in their respective causes. Expressions of support or opposition were secured from virtually every segment of the community. In most instances, participation was limited to formal endorsement or condemnation of the proposed plan. Only a minority of these groups and individuals later took an active part in the campaign. For most of them, the issues were too far removed from their main interests to elicit active involvement and the commitment of scarce resources. Yet, as is generally believed, the endorsement technique can be highly useful when the matter to be decided at the polls is complex and difficult to clarify for the average voter—and certainly the district proposal was not simple. In such cases an appeal to "authority"—to the collective judgment of the organization as expressed by its leaders—often serves as a substitute for personal understanding.

Lined up on the side of the proponents were the major business organizations of the area, the churches, professional societies, civic groups, and the metropolitan dailies. Arrayed against them were organized labor, the politicians, the County League of Municipalities, the weekly press, and the diminishing farmers of the county. Each group needs further comment.

The business leadership of the community, with few exceptions, supported

[2] *St. Louis Post-Dispatch,* October 8, 1959.

the district plan. Civic Progress, Incorporated early endorsed it as did both the city and county chambers of commerce and the heads of many leading St. Louis firms. The large business interests traditionally favored metropolitan reorganization, partly because they believe that the present fragmented system is not conducive to orderly and efficient administration, partly because they feel that reform will result in a better business and industrial climate, and partly because the development of their civic image requires them to promote such causes. The last motive appeared to be most prevalent among the business-men supporting the district proposal. Many of the business leaders were only mildly interested in the proposed charter, viewing it neither as a desirable necessity nor as a threat. Yet, if for no other reason, their position in the community compelled them to voice approval of a civic proposal endowed with such respectable sponsorship.

A number of the religious groups also announced their support of the plan. Among those formally endorsing it were the Metropolitan Church Federation of Greater St. Louis and the Missionary Baptist Pastors and Ministers Union Conference, an organization of Negro clergymen. The Catholic hierarchy made no announcement, but the official Catholic weekly of the archdiocese editorially supported the proposal and expressed the wish that its readers would vote favorably on it. No Jewish association took an official stand, but a prominent rabbi gave personal endorsement. These expressions of support by religious groups were not surprising or particularly significant in the light of local tradi-tion. It had long been common practice for the St. Louis churches to endorse movements for civic improvement, and the present campaign fell in that general category.

Although most of the trade and professional organizations remained neutral, a few such as the Realtors Association and the local chapters of the American Institute of Planners and the Institute of Architects publicly supported the proposal. Because of their concern with land use, each of these groups— realtors, planners, and architects—had something of a vocational or professional interest in the planning provisions of the charter.

The major civic organizations of the metropolitan area were also found in the ranks of the proponents. The ever-active League of Women Voters, including the suburban chapters, not only endorsed the charter but campaigned for its adoption. Other area-wide civic groups favoring the plan included the American Association of University Women, the Citizens Council on Housing and Community Planning, the General Council on Civic Needs, and the St. Louis Crime Commission. Local or sectional organizations such as improve-ment associations and neighborhood councils evidenced little public interest. Only three groups in this category took positions: two from the county in opposition and one from the city in favor.

The two metropolitan dailies, the *Post-Dispatch* and *Globe-Democrat*, gave full support to the district plan. Their news columns comprehensively covered all phases of the campaign while their editorial pages hammered away on the merits of the proposed charter. Starting in September the *Post-Dispatch* carried favorable editorials every four or five days. This pace was gradually stepped up until campaign editorials appeared daily during the two weeks prior to the election. Over this same period, Bill Mauldin's cartoon skills were utilized on eight different occasions. The *Globe-Democrat* followed a similar course but with less frequency. During the final week of the campaign both papers carried a huge banner headline in red ink across the top of the front page: VOTE YES ON METROPOLITAN DISTRICT PROPOSAL TUESDAY.

THE LINE-UP AGAINST

Organized labor was preponderantly against the district plan. It has always felt that its local political strength would be better enhanced through governmental consolidation than other types of reorganization. Labor's opposition to the district plan apparently grew out of the conviction, nurtured by Ferris and its other freeholder delegates, that a federal-type system would only delay or prevent the attainment of consolidation. The position of the union members on the Board of Freeholders had presaged labor's later stand, but it is doubtful that these representatives had been committed to total opposition. In fact, some top union officials had previously indicated to the survey staff that they were not averse to the district approach although they considered merger the ideal solution.

The most significant unit of labor to declare its opposition was the St. Louis Labor Council, representing virtually all labor unions in the area. Other influential labor voices included the International Union of Electrical Workers, the Communications Workers of America, and the International Association of Machinists. However, some labor support, most of it from the old craft unions, such as the Building and Construction Trades Council, did go to the district proponents. This was not the first occasion on which the leadership of these unions had differed with the majority position of labor on civic issues.

The central committees of the political parties in both city and county refrained from taking any stand on the grounds that the issue was not a partisan one. Within the city ward organizations, the personal influence of Cervantes and others on the citizens committee produced endorsements by 3 of the 28 Democratic ward organizations. Two Republican wards also announced support. In the remainder of the wards no official position was taken by either party. All but a few of the ward leaders appeared indifferent to the election and those who announced their support made no great effort to deliver. In the county, despite official neutrality, the situation was quite different. Leaders of both parties were actively opposed to the plan. County Democrats wanted no part of any arrangement that would align them closer to their city counterparts in local governmental affairs. County Republicans, on the other hand, shuddered at the thought of an agency that might open the door to further Democratic encroachment on local offices. Numerous township officials of both parties quietly but effectively worked against the plan at the "grass roots" level while area political leaders contented themselves with formal denunciations of the proposal.

Opposition was also active among officials at the municipal level. While the mayors of several large suburban cities spoke in favor of the district plan, the overwhelming percentage of local office holders were against it. Most municipal officials who endorsed the plan were part-time officeholders who held executive positions or operated businesses in the central city. Despite the efforts of these individuals, the County League of Municipalities unanimously adopted a resolution of opposition with the supporters abstaining.

St. Louis County still has some agricultural land in its outer reaches although the total acreage is rapidly dwindling. Farmers in expanding metropolitan areas have always looked with suspicion upon attempts to change the local governmental structure, and those in the St. Louis environs have been no exception. It came as no surprise, therefore, when the St. Louis County Farm Bureau, with 200 members, voted unanimously to oppose the plan.

In contrast to the metropolitan dailies, the community or neighborhood weeklies took strong positions against the district proposal. Of the 29 such papers in the area (the majority of them in the suburbs), 22 expressed opposition and the others remained silent. Three of the neighborhood newspapers, strategically located in various sections of the area, took the unusual step of publishing a series of special Sunday editions attacking the plan and warning their readers of the "fallacious" arguments being used in its behalf by the metropolitan press. Typical of their observations is the following simplified reasoning in opposition to the district proposal:

Whatever "metropolitan problems" exist or may arise as anyone well knows are of a peculiarly local nature. That holds true whether they are in the city, in the county or in any one of the county's incorporated areas. Local governments we strongly believe are best able to cope with them and we see no need whatever to set up a district layer of government to do the job.[3]

The community papers in suburban St. Louis have long been characterized by a strong anticentral-city bias and an equally strong antimetropolitan-press attitude. (In this latter respect they are joined by their neighborhood counter-

[3] *St. Louis County Observer*, September 9, 1959.

parts in the central city.) The adamant and provincial stand of the suburban papers in matters of metropolitan concern is consistent with these two biases. It is also consistent in the minds of their publishers with good business practice. Protecting the virtues of the small community against the encroachment and evils of the big city provides them with a worthy, and at times dramatic, cause. And by fighting the "outsider," they are less likely to step on the toes of their local constituency. Metropolitan reorganization seems particularly worrisome to them probably because they feel that it may in some way pose a threat to their existence.

Governmental reorganization movements in other metropolitan areas have often run afoul of attacks by organized "hate" groups. For example, literature pinning the communist label on sponsors of metropolitan reform movements appeared during the Dade County, Knoxville, and Nashville campaigns of recent years. In St. Louis the only incident of this sort was a reprinting without comment in a county newspaper of the notorious "Terrible 1313" article that originally appeared in the *American Mercury*. This article was aimed at the professional public administration organizations headquartered at 1313 E. 60th Street, Chicago. It castigated them as "swift moving teams of social engineers ... who operate through a radical political apparatus called Metro or Metropolitan Government."[4]

THE TUCKER STAND

The most crippling blow to the district plan was the "defection" of Mayor Raymond Tucker of St. Louis City. Tucker was by far the best-known political leader in the area. His stature and prestige were high in both city and county even though his close ties with the business community did not endear him to organized labor or the Negro. Tucker's position on the plan was not made known until shortly before the election, although his coolness toward it had been evident for some time. Shortly after publication of the survey report in August 1957, he had praised it in general terms, calling it an "excellent comprehensive study" that could serve as a guide in solving the area's problems. He made no mention, however, of the recommendation for a metropolitan district government. Later, during the hearings by the freeholders, he indicated that his ideal choice would be total merger, but since this was currently unattainable his practical choice was a return of the city into the county. Such a solution would be fiscally advantageous to the city because it would shift some welfare costs to the county and also abolish certain "county" offices that were saddled on the city by statute.[5]

[4] Jo Hindman, "Terrible 1313," *American Mercury*, January 7, 1959.

[5] The city as a county has certain statutory offices such as sheriff, coroner, and collector, which cannot be abolished by revision of the city charter.

In view of Tucker's prolonged silence and his evident lack of enthusiasm for the district approach, few observers expected him to endorse the plan. The question in their minds was whether he would publicly declare his opposition or take a neutral position. His most influential backers, the members of Civic Progress, Incorporated as well as other community elite and civic groups who had consistently supported him were on record as favoring the proposal. Heretofore they had always worked hand in hand with him on matters of civic concern, such as public-improvement bond issues, redevelopment projects, and charter revision. Now an obvious difference of opinion had arisen between them. Some key community leaders close to the mayor tried to persuade him to remain neutral at least. Others more politically minded endeavored to convince him that he would be the ideal choice for chief executive of the new government, but Tucker, already in his early sixties, apparently had no desire to embark on such a new and untried venture at this late stage in his public career.

On October 3, one month before the election, Tucker broke his silence with a carefully reasoned statement announcing his opposition to the plan. Calling it unsound and inefficient, he argued that it failed to reflect the economic, social, and cultural interdependence of the area. Among other criticisms, he objected to the omission of many metropolitan-type functions, the failure to reduce the number of governmental units, the increase in complexity of responsible area-wide government, and the continuance of "separateness of the City and County."[6] He contended that too much had been claimed for the plan, that it was too weak an instrument for carrying out the tasks assigned to it. "I fear," he said, "that adoption of the plan would be followed by widespread voter disillusionment and apathy toward further metropolitan area political reform." His statement concluded with a hopeful expression that should the voters reject the plan as he proposed, there were "a variety of fronts" on which to press for improvement. And with an ironic mention of the survey, he added that the survey report would provide "valuable guidelines" for future planning.

Tucker's opposition was damaging to the plan even among county voters in the higher socioeconomic scales who were more influenced by his position than by the views of their own local officials. In attacking the proposal, the mayor chose to disagree with those most closely identified with him and his projects over the years and to place himself on the side of those groups—political and labor—who had not been particularly friendly toward him. A number of reasons prompted his choice, probably the most important of which was the conviction (held in common by large central-city mayors) that political merger is the only satisfactory solution to the metropolitan problem and that lesser remedies will only weaken the position of the core city and dilute its powers. Conceivably, too, he might have been influenced by the likelihood, feared by

[6] Statement issued by the mayor's office, October 3, 1959.

central-city mayors, that reorganization schemes based on local federalism will create a powerful rival for the area's top political honors in the person of a metropolitan executive.

Other factors also influenced the mayor. In 1954 he had vigorously supported the creation of the Metropolitan Sewer District but the early tribulations that befell this experience in district organization had caused some public disillusionment. In August 1957, several weeks prior to the referendum on a new city charter championed by Tucker and the civic elite, the sewer district officials announced a substantial increase in service rates. Opponents of charter revision had seized on this irrelevant issue in order to discredit supporters of the new document. The sewer rate increase was regarded by some, including the mayor, as a contributory factor in the charter's defeat, and from this time on, Tucker appeared to develop a more hostile attitude to metropolitan plans, especially to any district approach.

A third but less tangible factor in shaping the mayor's decision was his attitude toward the original leaders in the citizens committee. It was known at the time the movement was launched that Tucker was irked at Cervantes for trying to assume the role of a metropolitan statesman. Later in the mayoralty race of 1957, Tucker's Republican opponent, Richard Mehan, charged that the mayor had failed to furnish leadership in the most important task facing St. Louis, that of intergovernmental cooperation between city and county. "It was Alderman A. J. Cervantes," Mehan pointed out, "who started the movement for city-county coordination two years ago by circulating petitions for the creation of a board of freeholders to study the problem." Remarks of this kind were not calculated to increase the mayor's warmth for the present movement. Cervantes, moreover, continued to be a prominent force in the campaign for the district plan, and its adoption would bring much credit to him as the "father" of the new government.

WAGING THE CIVIC BATTLE

Despite the interest expressed by pressure groups and leaders and the exhortations of the press, the campaign was a curious phenomenon characterized more by inactivity and apathy than by vigor and action. As Cervantes remarked shortly before the election, "This damned campaign never got off the ground." It was as though the proponents were not seriously committed to winning while the opponents were confident that the plan did not have a chance. Yet here was an issue presented to the electorate that could radically change the future course of government in a major metropolis. Few citizens seemed aware of the implications.

The proponents of reform relied heavily on the services of a public relations firm and discussion forums. Raising over $70,000 through contributions largely from members of Civic Progress, Incorporated and other business leaders, the City-County Partnership Committee publicized the plan through various mass media and literature, secured and disseminated endorsements by groups and influential individuals, organized "information" meetings, and sent speakers throughout the area to debate the merits of the proposal. Handicapped by the lack of any existent ward and township organizations to assist in reaching the grass roots, the committee tried with little success to form teams of workers at the local level. Funds of $500 per ward were also offered to party committeemen to pay workers in those instances where the party organization endorsed the plan, but because only a few city wards and no county townships placed their official blessings on the proposal, this expenditure was minimal and had little impact.

Most of the influential people who endorsed the plan lent their names and financial support but then took no further part in the campaign. One of the key individuals in Civic Progress, Incorporated contributed $2,500 to the committee and then left on an extended vacation. Others in the organization of businessmen behaved similarly, none of them assuming an active role in the campaign. Apparently never fully sold on the plan or the need for it, they completely withdrew from all but nominal participation when they learned of Tucker's opposition.

The inactivity of the business elite in favor of the proposal left the burden of directing the campaign to a relatively small number of individuals of lesser stature, mainly those from the ranks of the original citizens movement. The freeholders, who might have been in the forefront of the battle, were so evenly divided that the two factions neutralized each other, to the bewilderment of the voter. A few of the freeholders, such as Purteet and Buder, made numerous public appearances in behalf of the plan while others, such as Shewmaker and Mrs. Deakin, spoke against it. Still others, including Vatterott and McClellan, remained conspicuously silent. The League of Women Voters did conduct a telephone campaign to get out the vote and the St. Louis City Junior Chamber of Commerce stationed its members along major traffic arteries leading into the downtown area with large banners urging a favorable vote, but these efforts were the exception.

Opponents of the plan displayed no greater activity. The promergerite group—Citizens against the District Plan—expended $8,800, mostly contributed by organized labor, on the preparation and distribution of printed materials, and automobile stickers. The Webster Groves Task Force for Self-government spent less than $500, and the defenders of the status quo, the Citizens Committee for Self-government, functioned with virtually no expenditure. Each of these groups operated in isolation from the other and from individual opponents such as Tucker and the recently elected county supervisor,

James McNary. No massive "conspiracy" to defeat the plan existed—and those opposed saw little necessity for such unity.

With several notable exceptions, personal involvement was minimal by the opponents. Mayor Tucker, after his announcement of opposition, made only two talks against the plan. McNary, after condemning the proposal as one that would "saddle our citizens with another layer of government," engaged in no further opposition activity. Even the leaders of the merger group, the Citizens Committee against the District Plan, were not active. None of the three cochairmen made more than one public pronouncement after their original statement. Labor leaders were likewise quiescent, giving no indication of intensive campaigning.

In the county, the Citizens Committee for Self-government showed greater concern. In early October it announced a series of 26 mass meetings in opposition to the plan. The extent of public apathy is illustrated by the attendance at the meetings; most of them had to be cancelled for lack of an audience. One was "well attended"—it drew 55 persons, and this was in suburban Brentwood where the mayor was a leader of the opposition group.

At the grass-roots level, the opposition functioned far more effectively than the proponents, principally because in the party organizations it had a ready mechanism for mobilizing voter action. Particular use was made of this machinery in the county, where the local politicians and officeholders viewed the plan as a threat to their interests. In many townships the party committeemen worked against the proposal. In the city, although the politicians were overwhelmingly opposed to the plan, few ward leaders thought it necessary to mount precinct campaigns. Some of them in the "delivery" wards simply let their opposition be known and then turned their attention to "more important" matters.

METROPLEX ASSEMBLY

One unusual technique employed by a neutral source to inform the voter during the campaign is worthy of note. While the survey was still in progress, the local educational television station, KETC, presented a series of programs exploring metropolitan problems. Following the creation of the Board of Freeholders, it then televised a large number of that group's public meetings. Later, when the charter campaign got underway, the station's facilities were used in a unique attempt to acquaint the electorate with the proposed plan. The program was set up and executed by the Civic Education Center at Washington University with financial assistance from the Fund for Adult Education.

Known as Metroplex Assembly, the program included a number of steps. First, a series of meetings were held on cooperation with various civic and neighborhood groups in the area. Eleven of these took place during the summer months of 1959. Each meeting was moderated by a staff member from the center. One speaker favoring the district plan and one opposed to it were given equal time to present their cases. The rest of the meeting was devoted to questions and comments from the audience, which ranged in size from 40 to 200. These questions then formed the basis for the television discussions which followed later.

As the second phase of the program, the center organized approximately 400 "viewing posts" in private homes, each consisting of approximately 10 viewers. Hosts or discussion leaders for these posts were oriented as to methods and procedures in special institutes held by the center staff during the summer. The third and final step involved the use of television. Beginning in early October and continuing weekly until the election, particular aspects of the plan were presented over KETC by supporters and opponents. Those at the viewing posts were given briefing sheets prepared by the center for each program. After the television presentation, the viewers spent the next hour in discussion. Guests who had appeared on the earlier televised portion of the program then returned to the air and responded to questions and comments phoned in from the viewing posts.

This experiment in public information pointed up the widespread lack of knowledge about the plan among even the fairly intelligent citizenry. Many of the questions posed by the audience indicated total confusion. As the director of the center commented about the public meetings, "They were successful but sobering." The same pattern of confusion and uncertainty was evident at other public debates on the proposal. The plan was obviously complex, as any scheme of governmental federation may be, and this complexity played into the hands of the opposition. When the proponents could not quickly or simply rebut the claims of those attacking the plan, the voter received an unfavorable impression of its worthiness.

CAMPAIGN ISSUES

The civic debate over the reorganization proposal generated numerous issues, some legitimate, others spurious; some of import, others of petty concern. The proponents based their case on the common dogmas of metropolitan governmental reform: the inability of individual communities to cope with area-wide problems, such as traffic and transportation; the stifling effects of the existing system on the economic progress of the areas as demonstrated by "its failure to keep pace with comparable urban centers"; and the need for over-all guidance and direction in planning the area's future. The opposition presented two different arguments. Promergerites admitted the problems but contended that the proposed remedy was wholly inadequate; the status quo faction denied most of the problems and asserted that only minor adjustments were necessary for those that did exist.

YOU TAKE ME . . . AND I'LL "TAKE" YOU

St. Louis County Observer, Maplewood, Mo., September 30, 1959.

In addition to the dichotomous consolidation and home-rule arguments, two issues raised by the opposition had strong voter impact: taxes and a new level of government. Both recurred frequently during the campaign and both were used effectively in attacks on the plan. Any mention of new or increased taxes is a favorite theme of those opposing governmental innovation, a theme the average voter understands. Adoption of the reorganization proposal, opponents charged, would mean an increase in taxes. Pointing to the provision that would permit the new agency to levy a general property tax up to 50 cents on each $100 of assessed valuation, the impression was given that the homeowner's property tax would automatically be raised by that amount. Proponents

"NOW DON'T GET STUCK ON THE FIRST PAGE."
Mauldin in the *St. Louis Post-Dispatch*, August 10, 1959.

countered by explaining that the net increase in property taxes would not be large because the district would reduce local governmental expenses and local taxes by relieving local units of certain responsibilities. Supporters also cited the improved services that would accrue, noting that "We get what we pay for."

Taxpayers, however, are strangely immune to such arguments, and many voters were convinced that adoption of the district would mean a substantial tax increase.

The second issue was equally difficult to dispute. Opponents kept reiterating the idea that the plan would impose "a new layer of government while eliminating none now in existence." Proponents rejoined that no new layer was being created because a metropolitan district government already existed in the form of the sewer district, and that the plan did no more than expand and improve a government already in being. This argument, however, proved less than convincing to the voters, probably because many of them were unfavorably impressed by the sewer district.

A third, but spurious, issue was also raised in the county. The impression was given by some opponents that adoption of the plan would also alter or in some way affect the county school districts. Because the integrity of local school districts is a matter close to the hearts of many St. Louis Countians, even the erroneous intimation that the proposed reorganization scheme might somehow affect their school system was persuasive.

FIVE

/

The Vote

When the ballots were counted on November 3, the outcome was as most observers had expected: an overwhelming rejection of the metropolitan charter by the electorate. In the city the vote was two to one against (43,478 to 21,343); in the county three to one (82,738 to 27,633). Only 20 percent of the registered voters in the city and 40 percent in the county had participated in the election.

For purposes of analyzing the returns, the voting was examined in the light of two variables: socioeconomic status and extent of political party activity. Each of these variables was considered in relation to rate of electoral participation and direction of vote. Because of data deficiencies and limited research resources only rough approximations were made of these measurements. The results, although crude, throw some light on voting behavior in a metropolitan reorganization election.

VOTER TURNOUT AND SOCIAL RANK

Evidence concerning socioeconomic factors as related to voter turnout and support of local issues has failed to yield the precise cleavages reported for national and other partisan contests.[1] The vote on the St. Louis district plan once

[1] Analysis of the extensive citizens-attitude poll conducted by the survey indicates that measures reflecting socioeconomic stratification do not have nearly the predictive power regarding local election voting that they do in national contests. (See John C. Bollens, ed., *Exploring the Metropolitan Community*, Berkeley, Calif.: University of California Press, 1961, p. 225).

51

again underscores the difficulty of arriving at conclusions of predictive value in elections of this type. We normally would assume, for example, that rate of voter participation is closely correlated with socioeconomic status. Yet in the county returns on the district referendum, the lowest rate of participation occurred in the central portion of the area where the highest social rankings are found. Here only 37 percent of the registered voters went to the polls compared to 40 percent in the northern and 42 percent in the southern townships. The latter two areas are heavily weighted with socioeconomic scores in the middle range but they also contain a large number of blue-collar and lower-income communities.

When participation is broken down by township and related to social rank, the unevenness of the results is still manifest.[2] As Table 5 indicates, the percentage of townships showing a rate of participation higher than the county average of 39.9 is the same for each of the social categories, and while top honors went to a high ranking township with a voter turnout of 46.3 percent, the lowest participation in the county (32.5 percent) was recorded by another in the same socioeconomic class.

The city's participation pattern was closer to expectation. All four wards with highest social scores exceeded the city-wide turnout of 20.2 percent with an average rate of approximately 27 percent (see Table 6). The predominantly Negro wards, all in the lower social rank, were far below the city total with an

TABLE 5

CLASSIFICATION OF COUNTY TOWNSHIPS
BY SOCIAL RANK AND VOTING PARTICIPATION ON DISTRICT PLAN

Social rank	Above-average participation rate	Below-average participation rate	Total
High	2 (50%)	2 (50%)	4 (100%)
Middle	4 (50%)	4 (50%)	8 (100%)
Low	2 (50%)	2 (50%)	4 (100%)

[2] For purposes of analysis the county townships and city wards were divided into high, middle, and low categories on the basis of social rank (education and occupation) scores previously developed by the survey for census tracts with the use of the Shevky-Bell formula. (See *Background for Action*, St. Louis: Metropolitan St. Louis Survey, February 1957, pp. 11–18.) Arbitrary adjustments were made in those cases where the tracts do not conform to ward and township boundaries.

TABLE 6

CLASSIFICATION OF CITY WARDS BY
SOCIAL RANK AND VOTING PARTICIPATION ON DISTRICT PLAN

Social rank	Above-average participation rate	Below-average participation rate	Total
High	4 (100%)	0	4 (100%)
Middle	8 (80%)	2 (20%)	10 (100%)
Low	3 (21.5%)	11 (78.5%)	14 (100%)

average rate of less than 12 percent. The seven lower-income white wards, three of them above the city total, showed a participation rate of 19 percent, and while the socioeconomic characteristics of these latter two groups of wards are not altogether similar, Negro participation was below the rest of the population even when occupation and education are held constant. In the middle-range wards, the turnout rate was 23 percent, with eight of the ten in this category above the city average.

The extent of voter participation on the district plan was in marked contrast to the two earlier St. Louis elections on metropolitan reorganization propositions. In each of these previous instances, voter turnout in the city exceeded that in the county. On the 1954 sewer-district proposal, 45 percent of the registered electorate in the city cast ballots as contrasted to 30 percent in the county. Only a handful of voters went to the polls the following year when the transit plan was at issue, but even here the proportion of voters in the city (10 percent) exceeded that of the county (8 percent). The sewer-district proposal had the support of Mayor Tucker and the political parties in both areas. The mayor's strong endorsement had undoubtedly helped to boost the city total, but this factor alone fails to account for the much smaller turnout in the county where most of the sewage problems existed.

Unlike the sewer proposal, the transit election took place in an atmosphere of almost complete indifference. Both Tucker and the county supervisor announced opposition to the plan but neither campaigned actively against it. Actually, the proposal presented to the voters was so "watered down" and innocuous that few cared whether it passed or failed. The changes it contained would have upset no one; neither would they have met the transportation problem. Because all three measures—sewer, transit, and multidistrict—were voted on at special elections, participation was not influenced by other issues or contests on the ballot.

It is difficult to explain why city residents would be less motivated to take part in the district government election than in the balloting on the sewer proposal. One might speculate that central-city voters generally have little interest in movements for metropolitan reform short of merger and that they respond only when their political leaders make a major issue of the proposed change. What, in other words, would have been the effect on voter turnout in the city had Mayor Tucker and party officials been as vigorous in their opposition to the district charter as they had been in support of the sewer plan? One might also speculate with reference to the county vote that suburbanites—and perhaps voters in general—are less prone to go to the polls when they favor a governmental change then when they regard it as a possible threat to their interests. Most St. Louis Countians had favored creation of the sewer district as a remedy for a serious problem confronting them. Conversely, in the present campaign many of them may have been so impressed by the "loss of local autonomy" argument which suburban politicians skillfully exploited that they came to believe the proposed new government would jeopardize their way of life.

VOTER TURNOUT AND PARTISAN ACTIVITY

No clear-cut pattern emerges when rate of participation in the metropolitan-charter election is related to political party activity. In the five city wards where the plan had party endorsement, the turnout averaged only 17 percent. Three of these, however, are Negro wards, and in each the participation rate was slightly above the average of all Negro wards but not enough to be significant. In the two other wards, the turnouts (24.8 percent and 26.7 percent) were substantially above the city-wide average and also above those for their own social-rank groupings.

The county pattern is somewhat more indicative although the information on extent of political party activity is not sufficient to warrant definitive conclusions. In the four townships where active opposition by the party organization is known to have taken place, the turnout was either close to or above the county average. This finding is more significant than the figures reveal because each of these townships is in the low social-rank group. Partial explanation for the failure of the county turnout rate to correlate more closely with socioeconomic status may be attributed to differences in degree of partisan activity among the townships.

DIRECTION OF VOTE AND SOCIAL RANK

Numerous election studies have shown that education and occupation, or social rank, are closely related to the direction of the vote in partisan contests. Much less scrutiny has been given to voting behavior in elections on local issues. The work thus far undertaken in this area indicates a positive correlation between social rank and voting for such measures as charter revision or governmental reorganization.[3] This pattern was manifest in the vote on the sewer-district plan when both city and county voting followed the expected configuration, with areas of high social attributes recording higher percentages in favor of the proposals than the low ranking sections.[4]

A similar pattern is observable in the direction of the vote on the metropolitan charter. Because only two city wards and no county townships recorded majorities for the plan, the median percentages in each jurisdiction favoring the proposal (30.3 percent in the city and 20.7 in the county) were used to differentiate areas that gave above-average support from those below the average. As Tables 7 and 8 show, the gross measure employed in the analysis supports the common assumption that voters of high social rank tend to favor metropolitan reorganization proposals more than do those lower on the continuum. The vote in both city and county conformed generally to the anticipated patterns. Seven of the eight high-ranking electoral units in the two jurisdictions recorded favorable votes above the median compared to eight of eighteen middle and seven of eighteen low-ranking wards and townships.

TABLE 7

CLASSIFICATION OF CITY WARDS BY
SOCIAL RANK AND DIRECTION OF VOTE
ON DISTRICT PLAN

Social rank	Above median voting "Yes"	Below median voting "Yes"	Total
High	3	1	4
	(75%)	(25%)	(100%)
Middle	4	6	10
	(40%)	(60%)	(100%)
Low	7	7	14
	(50%)	(50%)	(100%)

[3] See, for example, Edward B. Olds and David W. Salmon, *St. Louis Voting Behavior Study,* St. Louis: Metropolitan St. Louis Census Committee, 1948.

[4] See W. C. Kaufman and Scott Greer, "Voting in a Metropolitan Community," *Social Forces,* March 1960.

TABLE 8

CLASSIFICATION OF COUNTY TOWNSHIPS BY
SOCIAL RANK AND DIRECTION OF VOTE ON
DISTRICT PLAN

Social rank	Above median voting "Yes"	Below median voting "Yes"	Total
High	4 (100%)	0	4 (100%)
Middle	4 (50%)	4 (50%)	8 (100%)
Low	0	4 (100%)	4 (100%)

Whether a meaningful relationship exists between extent of participation and direction of vote on metropolitan-reform issues has also been the subject of speculation. Most observers feel that the probability of success in such elections is enhanced by a heavy vote. Others, however, argue that a small vote is more conducive to a favorable verdict. The latter position assumes an inverse ratio between size of vote and proportion of upper social-rank participants and a high positive correlation between social rank and the direction of the vote. The St. Louis election throws little light on either of these views except to show their precarious status. Within the city, a significant rank-order correlation of +0.581 was found between rate of participation and "yes" votes, but in the county the correlation (+0.104) between these two variables was insignificant. It is possible that the larger than expected rate of participation by lower-ranking county voters as compared to those in the higher categories distorted the normal relationship between turnout and direction of vote. If so, the case of those who equate success in metropolitan reform with a large vote is strengthened.

DIRECTION OF VOTE AND PARTISAN ACTIVITY

The returns on the St. Louis district proposal also indicate the influence of political party activity. It will be observed in Table 7 that the percentage of city wards of low social rank favoring the plan is greater than that in the middle range. This is the only point of deviation in both city and county from the expected voting pattern. In two of the seven low-status wards with "yes" votes above the city median the plan had party endorsement, and in a third the Democratic committeeman was personally friendly to Cervantes and his cause even though no formal position was taken by the organization.

Partisan influence is also evident in the middle-range rankings where the only ward in which the proposal received party endorsement recorded the highest percentage of favorable votes among the units in this group. More activity probably took place in this ward, which is Cervantes' home base, than in the others. Similar indication of the effect of party-organization support appears in the high social-rank category. Two wards in this group voted in favor of the plan. In one the proposal passed with a 74 percent favorable vote; in the other it carried by 62 percent. In the first instance the proposal had partisan support; in the second no party endorsement was made. Because the two wards are similar in socio-economic characteristics, political activity in the first most likely contributed to its substantially higher percentage of favorable votes.

On the negative side, evidence of the impact of partisan opposition is also found. In the city ward where the plan suffered its worst defeat, with a vote of almost 7 to 1, the Democratic committeeman, Jordan Chambers, "quietly" opposed its passage. The ward is known as a "delivery" ward, and as one of the political leaders commented, "Chambers need not say anything; all he needs to do is let his views be known." Comparable results of political activity are also shown in the county returns. The four townships where partisan opposition was known to be the most intense recorded the smallest percentage of favorable votes cast in any of the suburban districts. In these four units the plan was defeated by an average vote of nearly 8 to 1. In one district where the committee-man, an influential figure in county Democratic politics, has long been openly hostile to any form of metropolitan reorganization, the proposal lost by a margin of 11 to 1. The participation rate in this township was also among the highest in the entire city-county area.

OTHER FACTORS

There are other factors in addition to social rank and partisan activity that help to explain some of the variations among the results in individual electoral districts. Several studies have noted a marked distinction in voting patterns when local issues of certain types are on the ballot between areas where voters rent their dwellings and those containing a large proportion of homeowners. A Seattle study, for example, disclosed that home and property owners are the most tax-conscious voters and tend to oppose measures that will increase taxes for changes not of direct and immediate benefit to the taxpayers.[5]

The St. Louis referendum shows similar trends. Of the four high-ranking city wards, the two in which the plan passed are in the west-central section of the community where a large number of medium- and high-rental apartments are located. The other two wards, in which the proposal failed of acceptance, are in

[5] See Calvin F. Schmid, *Social Trends in Seattle,* Seattle: University of Washington Press, 1944.

the predominantly single-family residential sections in the southwestern part of the city. In the wards of medium social rank where home ownership prevails the average favorable vote was below that for the city as a whole and even substantially below that for the low-income neighborhoods where rental units are common.

The county vote also manifests the influence of property ownership. Of the four upper-rank townships, three are in the central section of the county where a large number of high-rent apartments are found. The fourth is in the Webster Groves-Kirkwood area to the southwest where single-family units are almost universal. The favorable vote in the central townships averaged 42 percent while in the latter it was only 27 percent. No observation can be made as to the effect of this factor in the rest of the county without more selective analysis because home ownership prevails throughout, even in the lower-ranking communities.

It is likely, in view of the wide play given to the question of tax increases during the campaign, that this issue figured prominently in shaping the home-owner's attitude toward the district plan. It is likely also that home ownership engenders a greater feeling of commitment to one's neighborhood or subcommunity and thereby causes owner-voters to be more receptive to arguments depicting governmental change as a threat to neighborhood autonomy. If these assumptions are correct, the fact that the percentage of owner-occupied dwelling units in the city is less than half that of the county would help to explain the voting differential in the two areas.

An additional factor might also be noted. A large portion of the south county, although heavily urbanized, remains unincorporated. Residents in this section have traditionally opposed greater coordination with the central city or even with other governmental units in the county. By remaining unincorporated, they have managed to escape municipal taxation while at the same time receiving certain essential urban services from the county government—services that are financed out of general revenue and not by special charges. Many residents of these areas are therefore chary of all metropolitan reorganization plans as possible threats to their subsidized services. Some evidence of this attitude is found in the vote on the district proposal. In the urbanized townships that are predominantly unincorporated, the percentage of the vote against the plan was substantially larger than the county average.

SOME ELECTORAL CONCLUSIONS

Several general conclusions emerge from the analysis of the St. Louis vote. Although necessarily tentative because of the many variables involved in an election of this kind, they are highly suggestive. They are meant to apply, moreover, only to the federal-type plans for reorganization that are commonly recommended today. More drastic proposals, such as merger, would necessitate the reconstruction of several of these propositions.

1. Voter turnout on issues of metropolitan reorganization is correlated with social rank, but this relationship is an uneasy one and subject to alterations by other factors, such as partisan activity.

2. The direction of the vote is also correlated with social rank: individuals high on the scale are more apt to support area-wide reform than those of lower rank.

3. No clear relationship has as yet been established between extent of voter turnout and direction of vote.

4. Extent of voter participation increases with intensity of partisan activity.

5. The most effective opposition arguments in reorganization campaigns are tax increases and "supergovernment," or loss of local automony.

6. Apartment dwellers and renters are less susceptible than homeowners to the usual opposition arguments.

7. The most important factor in determining the direction of the vote is political support or opposition. No metropolitan plan *can* pass over the active opposition of the political parties. No such plan *is likely* to pass without active partisan support.

SIX

Metropolitan Post-Mortem

The St. Louis experiment adds to the long list of failures to win governmental reorganization battles in the nation's metropolitan areas. In retrospect, the movement could not possibly have succeeded. The forces at work against it were too powerful, and the groups for it too uncommitted to bring about the proposed changes. Reshaping the governmental pattern of the metropolis is a complex task that impinges upon a variety of change-resistant interests and clusters of power. The St. Louis election once again demonstrated the ease with which these interests can be mobilized into an effective army of opposition through use of the existing network of relationships among public officials and interest cliques. It also gave added emphasis to the shopworn truism that it will take more than metropolitan surveys and public pronouncements by the civic elite to modify the present system of local government in any significant fashion.

The welter of confusing facts and circumstances that surround a metropolitan reform effort such as that in St. Louis seems to defy analysis. Yet each of these attempts provides new insights, new perspectives, and hopefully better understanding of the political processes at work in our urban centers. The abortive St. Louis venture into the field of area-wide constitution making was not altogether in vain. From the standpoint of practical accomplishments it stimulated thinking and minor action on several problems and led to some governmental readjustments of lesser scope. More importantly, from the standpoint of knowledge it contributed to clearer understanding of several facets of the metropolitan-reorganization issue. This latter result is discussed within the framework of three questions:

60

1. Why was the degree of commitment or involvement by the majority of citizens and many major interest groups relatively low, and what effect did this factor have on the outcome of the referendum?

2. What impact did the comprehensive study conducted by the universities have on the charter drafters and the general public?

3. What are the minimum essentials or preconditions that must exist in a metropolitan area before broad-scale reorganization is possible?

THE PATHOLOGY OF METROPOLITAN ACTION PROGRAMS

Ironically, the metropolitan reorganization proposal in St. Louis was caught in a heavy cross fire from opposite extremes. On the one hand it was attacked because it was too timid; on the other, because it was too far-reaching. The uncongenial union of these two dichotomous forces is symptomatic of the factors that impede restructuring of metropolitan governmental patterns. There are always individuals and groups who see personal advantages and opportunities in changing the system. There are others who have vested interests in preserving the existing arrangements. Finally, there are still others who have no personal stake in the system other than that of citizens concerned with its proper operation. Supporters of metropolitan reform fall predominantly into this last category—a fact that helps to explain the weaknesses of the reorganization movement.

The most highly motivated proponents of change are those who anticipate personal rewards from a restructured system. If the prize is attractive enough, they are willing to commit time, money, and effort in order to achieve the desired alteration. Normally this group includes politicians and interest groupings of various economic, social, and racial dimensions. Those in this classification usually play negative roles in metropolitan reform. When not in active opposition, they have been lukewarm or neutral toward reorganization proposals. Their lack of enthusiasm can be explained by several factors, particularly the nature of the reform plans and the unresponsiveness of the general public.

For some years now, the common approach to metropolitan reorganization has been based on the gospel of management efficiency and the dogma of local autonomy tempered by the transfer of certain nonlocal powers to an area-wide agency. Discarding political consolidation as unrealistic or undesirable, the mid-twentieth-century movement to "save the cities" continues to view the metropolitan problem as essentially one of relating sound engineering and administrative solutions to matters of sewage disposal, traffic control, water supply, and like functions. And by concentrating its attention on organizational efficiency, reformist activity has assiduously avoided the deeper and more controversial

62

questions of the metropolis such as racial assimilation, housing, economic segregation, and even public education.

"IF YOU NEED ME, HONK."

Mauldin in the *St. Louis Post-Dispatch*, September 21, 1959.

The consequences of this approach are not difficult to ascertain. To couch metropolitan reform in purely administrative terms is to divorce it from those issues motivating large interest coalitions. These groups are unwilling to expend their resources on a cause that skirts the problems concerning them. On those occasions when they are enlisted in the cause by the proponents of reform, these interest groups give little more than nominal support. Similarly, when they are attracted into the ranks of the opposition, as in St. Louis, they put only minimal effort into the task.

A central-city mayor, a political party, and possibly labor may visualize distinct political rewards in a merger of local governments, but they normally see little payoff in lesser schemes. Cervantes deviated from the general behavior pattern of core-city politicians, perhaps because he saw in the reorganization movement an issue that would further his political ambitions. But Tucker and not Cervantes was the political leader of the area, a fact which seriously impeded Cervantes' ability to mobilize widespread support for metropolitan reform. Suburban politicians have likewise seen only risks and little reward in espousing the reorganization movement. Some of them at the county level have occasionally supported plans that utilize the county government as the metropolitan vehicle, but here again they are attracted by the anticipated rewards.

One major reason for the largely negative attitude of the political leaders and parties toward metropolitan reorganization lies in the unresponsiveness of the citizenry toward the issue. It is frequently assumed that the impetus for governmental change in metropolitan areas is generated by widespread dissatisfaction with services. But this great ground swell of popular dissatisfaction is more mythical than real. The direction of urban growth may be such as to "negate the rich promise of American life," but the average citizen remains unconvinced of this awesome possibility. In St. Louis, and more recently in Dayton, attitude surveys clearly demonstrated that most people are relatively well satisfied with their local governments and have few service complaints. St. Louis residents had no strong criticism of any of their governments. Only 1 unit of more than 150 was considered to be performing poorly by as many as 10 percent of the residents—and ironically, this was the sewer district, a metropolitan agency. In answer to questions about various local governmental services, only recreation, traffic, and transportation drew responses of dissatisfaction from more than 17 percent of those interviewed.[1]

The results in Dayton were similar. There, only about one in ten persons believed that his local government was poor in either efficiency or responsiveness to the people. Less than one half of the respondents had either felt like complaining or had complained about a local governmental service. Almost 60 percent could name no more than one service with which they were dissatisfied.[2] It is unrealistic to believe that those in charge of the local governmental machinery will support major changes under such circumstances. Until popular concern or dissatisfaction with the existing system is made more evident, few local political leaders can be expected to champion the cause of metropolitan govern-

---

[1] John C. Bollens, ed., *Exploring the Metropolitan Community,* Berkeley, Calif.: University of California Press, 1961, pp. 188–190.

[2] *Metropolitan Challenge,* Dayton: Metropolitan Community Studies, 1959, pp. 241–251.

ment. Many of them look upon it as an issue devoid of popular appeal. Some of them take advantage of it in a negative sense by assuming the role of St. George and protecting the "little governments" against the voracious dragon. Others portray themselves as political Pasteurs, defending the central city against the suburban parasites.

If party leaders generally and mass-based interest groups particularly evidence only mild concern over the reorganization issue, the same cannot be said for the administrative bureaucracy and the officeholders who have high personal stakes in the retention of the existing system. This group includes the central-city mayor as well as the suburban official. The first will accept an enhancement of his power through political merger but fight against a dilution of it by functional consolidation of selected services, such as envisaged by the St. Louis plan. The second looks with suspicion on all change as a possible threat to his interest. Only in those instances in which existing arrangements are damaging his position of leadership—a sewer or water crisis, for example—is he willing to accept minimal modification of the structure. It is the members of this officeholding group who are the most strongly motivated by the risks and rewards of metropolitan reform and usually the most active in campaigns involving this issue.

The third group—the civic reformers—includes the economic elite, the "good government" people, the metropolitan press, and a sprinkling of other community-minded individuals and organizations. The prize they seek is an efficient system of local government; there are few personal stakes. Even the economic leaders do not feel that a change in the existing system will enhance their business interests in any material fashion. Hence, while they are willing to play their role as symbols of civic virtue and champions of progressive local government, their motivation is seldom strong enough to commit them to an all-out effort for metropolitan reorganization.

This coalition of good-government forces and business is further handicapped in issues requiring popular referendum by lack of a constituency that can be readily mobilized. The group's effectiveness in winning electoral support is therefore severely limited unless it can entice into the cause such mass-based groups as the political parties and labor. The press is similarly handicapped. Although it has a mass audience, its ability to mobilize the public in a civic cause is restricted by the interests and predispositions of its readers, their readiness to listen, and their capacity to understand the issues.

A division somewhat parallel to the three categories of interest groups can also be identified among the general citizenry. These three types might be plotted on a continuum as mergerites, or metropolitanites, moderate integrationists, and local autonomists, or localists. They appear in sharp contrast in the attitude interviews conducted by the universities. The findings of the survey study prompted the conclusion in the final public report that a majority of both city and county residents "favor a plan of government that will vest control over area-wide functions in a metropolitan agency," [3] a conclusion that found little support in the election returns. The results of the interviews are of some relevancy here.

Respondents were presented with a simplified statement of the various alternatives for governmental change possible under existing laws and were asked if they liked or disliked each alternative. Retention of the status quo was included in the list. Although the variations in responses were not striking, the metropolitan-district system was the most generally favored (by 53.5 percent of those interviewed) and the status quo the most generally disapproved (54.4 percent). More significantly, however, were the responses to a succeeding question: "Which of these proposals do you like best and which do you dislike the most?" As Table 9 shows, a relatively high degree of polarization existed among the residents of the area with a majority (54.5 percent) preferring either total merger or no change in the existing system. The balance of the answers were divided among three proposals of a more moderate nature.

The respondents who preferred merger generally favored the status quo least, while a majority of the localists disliked merger most. Since the district system was the only alternative that elicited a clear majority of favorable responses to

TABLE 9

RESPONSES TO VARIOUS ALTERNATIVES FOR GOVERNMENTAL CHANGE
IN ST. LOUIS AREA
(EXPRESSED IN PERCENTAGES)

Proposal	Liked this proposal most	Disliked this proposal most
Merger of all governmental units	33.5	26.9
Consolidate the two county governments but retain all local units	13.4	13.8
Create a local federal system by establishing a metropolitan district government	15.3	9.8
Consolidate the suburban municipalities into a smaller number	10.3	10.9
Leave present governments just as they are	21.0	28.8
Don't know	6.5	9.8
	100.0	100.0

[3] *Path of Progress,* St. Louis: Metropolitan St. Louis Survey, August 1957, p. 68.

the initial question of likes and dislikes, and since it was the least disliked of all the listed changes, it appeared to be the solution with the most political appeal. This analysis, however, did not anticipate the union of the two extremist groups—the metropolitanites and the localists. It wrongly assumed that a majority of those who favored merger most but did not express a dislike for the district plan would also accept the lesser solution.

The interviews suggest that those who favor complete consolidation and those who support the status quo are more firmly committed to these views than are the moderates to any particular lesser remedy. The latter, although expressing their general approval of a metropolitan district, were almost equally divided as to which intermediate proposal they liked best. These findings also suggest that the stronger commitment of those in the two polar positions will likely motivate them to greater activity than the moderates in a campaign for metropolitan reorganization. The situation might be summarized in this fashion: the localists are prone to resist any change of consequence; the metropolitanites are inclined to be hostile or disinterested in any proposal that does not embrace political merger; the moderates are likely to remain apathetic, confused, and uncertain as to the proper remedy.

Several interesting points of contrast between the St. Louis election and the Cuyahoga County (Cleveland) referendums serve to underscore these general observations and assumptions. On the same day that the St. Louis plan was submitted to the electorate, residents of Cuyahoga County rejected a metropolitan reorganization proposal (in the form of a county home-rule charter) that had been drafted by an official commission. Unlike the overwhelming defeat in St. Louis, the Cleveland charter was turned down by a much smaller margin, losing in the central city by approximately 29,000 votes out of 193,000 cast and in the remainder of the county by only 8,000 out of almost 226,000. Unlike the St. Louis proposal also, the Cleveland plan at least had the formal approval of the political parties while several top politicians, particularly those who stood to gain from a refurbished county government, worked actively for the charter. The business leaders also were active in support of the cause.

Leading the opposition in Cleveland, as in St. Louis, were the central-city mayor, the administrative bureaucracy, and suburban officialdom. The most active and effective campaigners among the opponents were the heads of two city departments whose functions were to be transferred to the county under the reorganization plan. Their colorful appeals repeatedly captured public attention away from the charter proponents.[4] The only large-scale interest bloc to oppose the plan actively was the Negro community which saw in it a threat to its growing political power within the central city. (In St. Louis the Negro opposition was much less active, possibly because the district proposal involved

[4] See E. E. Sparlin, "Cleveland Seeks New Metro Solution," *National Civic Review*, March 1960.

only functions of peripheral concern to the Negro leaders.) By enlisting the support of many of the politicians and motivating the civic leaders, the Cleveland plan made a better showing at the polls. It might have succeeded had the central-city mayor espoused it. The same cannot be said of the St. Louis charter.

THE SURVEY INFLUENCE

The St. Louis Board of Freeholders and the metropolitan charter election had been preceded by an extensive university study designed to ascertain the facts, identify the problems, and work out realistic remedies. Generously financed, this diagnostic and prescriptive study had been staffed by professionally competent personnel and conducted with civic approbation. The sponsorship was unimpeachable—both universities were highly respected in the community. Preceding sections of the present case study have already indicated that the survey's findings and recommendations greatly influenced the "moderate" faction on the Board of Freeholders, and that the plan ultimately presented to the voters was in effect the plan of the first researchers.

Members of the merger bloc on the board were not happy with the recommendations, and while they could not openly repudiate the study because of its prestigious sponsorship, they insisted from the beginning that the survey group could not be substituted for the freeholders' staff. This strategy of disassociation was evident throughout the board's deliberations, appearing particularly whenever survey staff members were called upon to testify. The attempt, however, was far from successful because the district bloc repeatedly referred to the survey report in support of its position. It is doubtful, in fact, that the district proposal could have prevailed in the board without the authority and rationale of the report in support of the position.

The dilemma posed here is one constantly faced by researchers whose findings will lead to specific proposals for action. Should such fact finders make recommendations that necessarily involve value judgments and assessments of political realities, or should they merely present the facts with possible alternative solutions? In the St. Louis case the recommendations of independent "experts" attached to no official or citizens' committee were presented to the public in anticipation of a charter commission. Following the report, a Board of Freeholders, presumably representative of the people, was called into existence to draft a plan of government. Members of the board whose judgments or views differed from those of the "experts" found themselves at a disadvantage in disputing the wisdom of a highly respected group.

Several freeholders in the promerger faction bitterly complained that the survey recommendations had placed the board in the unenviable position of ratifying an already formulated plan or risking public disapprobaticn for repudiating the universities. They contended that the survey report's disclaimer of intention to present a charter while offering "working proposals" for board consideration was meaningless—the fact is that a plan *was* presented and that it carried the imprimatur of the study group. In their view the survey staff should have confined itself to the assembling of facts and problems and left the board unhandicapped in order to perform its constitutional duty of determining which remedy should be presented to the people. As Shewmaker expressed it, "The people in their wisdom have decided that it is boards like ours rather than political scientists that are best able to make the decisions." But he continued plaintively, "I realize that to talk about political scientists at all is ... somewhat like talking about motherhood." [5]

The metropolitan expert's role, however, is not so simple as the mergerites describe it. As a specialist, he is expected not only to diagnose but also to prescribe for the ills of the community. Metropolitan reformers want this kind of assistance—not merely a delineation of problems. Had the survey limited itself to the role of the community's fact finder and not its mentor, it would have failed to meet the expectations of many of its supporters.

Although it is difficult to see how any metropolitan study can remain neutral in the recommendations, there are points at which a report can judiciously be uncommitted. The question of election types provides one such instance in the St. Louis plan. The survey's recommendation of nonpartisan elections for metropolitan councilmen and the chief executive was severely criticized by labor and political leaders, and the plan ultimately presented to the voters rejected the proposal in favor of partisan elections. By leaving questions of this type unanswered the survey could have avoided peripheral issues that diverted attention from the main recommendations and needlessly aroused opposition to or raised doubts about the survey in general.

Once the campaign got under way, the survey report was forgotten as an issue. Proponents of the plan referred to it in their talks and debates, and the metropolitan press often supported its editorials in behalf of the proposal by citing the "experts" on the survey staff. On the other side of the fence, a few extremists among the opposition spoke caustically of the survey, one of them remarking that it was "a shame the Ford Foundation could not have given $300,000 to an able group of people who would sincerely try to find what makes the multiplicity of governments work better and cheaper." [6] Other than these occasional references, there is no indication that the survey played an important role in the campaign. It is doubtful that a highly technical study of an exceedingly complex issue can have any direct influence on the mass of citizens. Its impact, if any, will be on the opinion formulators, and in the St.

[5] Transcript of meeting of the Committee of the Whole, Metropolitan Board of Freeholders, November 13, 1958.

[6] Quoted in the *St. Louis Globe-Democrat*, September 23, 1959.

Louis area many of these people were unwilling to accept the judgments of the survey because the proposals differed from their own views and interests.

A second question concerning the survey's impact relates to the character of the sponsorship. Is a university-conducted study designed as the basis for an action program actually an effective medium for action? Here further comparison with the Cleveland experience is helpful. As in St. Louis, the creation of an official charter commission in Cleveland had been preceded by a comprehensive study. Unlike the St. Louis survey, however, the Cleveland study was conducted under the direction of a lay citizens' board. Throughout the research period, every effort was made to secure wide community involvement in the work and to keep the public fully informed. Numerous subcommittees consisting of civic leaders, government officials, politicians, labor representatives, and businessmen were appointed to work with the professional staff. Over 250 influential citizens and public officials actively participated in the study groups.[7]

The Cleveland procedure ensured the existence of a large nucleus of influential community leaders who were wholly or partially committed to the findings and recommendations of the study and intellectually and emotionally prepared to push for action once the work was completed. The St. Louis study, on the other hand, was conducted with no formal public participation or citizen committees. Under this arrangement, the scholar was relieved of the task of educating and guiding a lay committee and bringing about consensus among its members. This approach afforded the researcher more time and greater freedom in order to make his basic study without using time on administrative or public relations work characteristic of many metropolitan surveys. That the research in the St. Louis venture profited and the subsequent action program suffered as a consequence is a likely hypothesis. While other factors, particularly strong political support, contributed to a more favorable vote in Cleveland, the campaign activity of the civic elite was considerably more pronounced there than in St. Louis—a participation no doubt encouraged by the active involvement of the community leaders in the research program.

METROPOLITAN PROGNOSIS

In both the St. Louis and Cleveland cases the reorganization plans met defeat in the central city as well as in the suburbs. Noteworthy also are two other defeats of reorganization proposals in the same year. In Knox County, Tennessee, a consolidation plan was decisively voted down by core-city residents and suburbanites; and in New Mexico a proposed merger of the City of Albu-

[7] For an account of the vast effort that went into this process, see J. A. Norton, "The Natural History of Metropolitan Surveys," paper delivered at the 1959 annual meeting of the American Political Science Association.

querque and Bernalillo County was similarly rejected by top-heavy votes both inside and outside the city. The chaste suburbs have generally been regarded as balky brides-to-be in metropolitan marriages but now the rakish central cities have also assumed the role of reluctant grooms. This series of setbacks may indicate that metropolitan governmental relations are becoming more inflexible, and that instead of progressing closer to agreement, the present pattern of local political pluralism had become institutionalized to the point where only catastrophe or the imminent threat of it will bring radical readjustment.

In addition to the usual handicaps, the metropolitan-reform movement in St. Louis suffers from other congenital defects. The long divorcement of the city from the county has created a traditional chasm of "separateness" that will be difficult to bridge. Mayor Tucker, for obvious fiscal reasons, would have been willing to see the city return to the county, but reentry itself offers no solution to the problems of the area. Although such an approach would provide a ready-made metropolitan vehicle in the form of the county government, it is highly improbable that Tucker and the central-city bureaucracy would consent to a power loss to this unit any more than they would to a metropolitan district. Use of the reentry proposal would have negated one telling argument used by the opposition—creation of an expensive new level of government—but it would have touched off another sensitive issue among suburban voters, that of saddling county residents with the fiscal burdens of the city.

The political isolation of the two jurisdictions has, moreover, created another disunifying element that militates against reentry or, for that matter, any other significant metropolitan remedy. Because of the legal division, each area has separate political party organizations, each with its own leadership structure and individual spheres of influence. As a result, leaders of both parties in the county look with disfavor on any arrangement that would throw them together structurally with the city organizations (as reentry presumably would). Enrollment of the political parties in the metropolitan-reform cause is thus a far more difficult task in St. Louis than in Cleveland or other areas where the party organizations are coterminous with the county.

A third impediment to governmental reorganization in St. Louis lies in the nature of the enabling provisions for adjusting city-county relations. Generally, a metropolitan area that has constitutional authorization to accomplish structural and functional reform on its own initiative is considered fortunate. However, the rigid demarcation and inflexibility of the alternatives open to the St. Louis reformers are more of a handicap than blessing. So long as the enabling grant exists, the natural tendency is to employ it rather than seek other constitutional or statutory authorization. Yet these provisions place those endeavoring to work out a satisfactory solution to the area's problems in a serious bind, as the deliberations of the freeholders so graphically illustrated. Had the board, for example, been able to use the county government as the metropolitan vehicle, the possibility of reaching broader agreement among its members would have been greatly enhanced—a possibility clearly indicated by the paired voting analyses. Reorganization under any circumstances involves legal problems; in metropolitan St. Louis these are blown up out of all proportion by the intricacies of the enabling provisions. Confusion and uncertainty among community leaders as well as the general public are the inevitable results.

Where then does all this leave the cause of metropolitan reform in the St. Louis area? When Cervantes was asked for his reactions to the defeat, he replied that the community simply was not "ready" for metropolitan government. He stated further that even if the proponents had spent several times as much as they had "the plan would still have been soundly defeated." In similar vein, another political leader observed that reorganization will be possible only when an obviously bad breakdown in existing local government occurs or when there is a manifest economic interest at stake for the voters. In the St. Louis case, the only acute problem of a readily visible nature was traffic, but traffic in St. Louis is no worse than in most other large metropolitan centers. Nor was there any immediate concern about the local economic situation. Proponents of reform did argue that the economic future of the area was being jeopardized by an irrational political structure with its inability to control growth, but most voters respond only to the economic facts of the present, and in 1959 these caused no alarm.

It is unlikely that any serious effort at comprehensive reorganization in the St. Louis metropolis will be instituted in the near future. Shortly after the district election, the promerger group announced plans to campaign for political consolidation, but few seemed to have any taste for this attempt and the movement soon dissipated. The picture, however, is not one of unmitigated bleakness. Progress in the form of lesser remedies will undoubtedly take place during the next decade—certainly a transit authority, partial reorganization of the county government, further school-district consolidation, and perhaps even merger of some suburban municipalities. But if broader reform is to be accomplished it will require far greater interest among the general citizenry than now exists, the support of key political leaders in both city and county, a genuine rather than token commitment on the part of the economic and civic elite, and assistance from some of the mass-based interest groups. That these conditions will materialize in the foreseeable future is a possibility highly remote.

Appendix

CONSTRUCTION OF MATRICES

Use of the paired agreement matrices to describe and analyze the political behavior of the freeholders has been adapted from the work of Rice, Beyle, Pritchett, Schubert, and Truman.[1] These social scientists have successfully used quantitative techniques for the analysis of small groups such as courts and legislative bodies. The methodology is based on the premise that bloc alignments in small groups are revealed in nonunanimous or divided votes among the members.

The matrices shown in the three tables in Chapter Three contain for all possible pairs of freeholders the percentages of instances in which they agreed with each other in the 36 nonunanimous roll-call votes during their year of deliberations. In determining these percentages the total agreements of each pairing of 18 freeholders was divided by the total number of possible agreements between each pair (excluding votes on which one or both were absent).

The order of the position in which the freeholders appear on the matrix scales was determined initially by their vote on the final choice of the plan. District adherents on the final vote are assigned the top nine places on the vertical scale in Table 1, and mergerites, the lower nine. The order is slightly different in the chronological divisions contained in Tables 2 and 3 because of Simmons' switch from a strong promerger stand during the first half of the board's life to an equally firm prodistrict bias during the latter half of its existence.

Within each of these two categories, district and merger, the order has been arbitrarily arranged on the matrices so that each freeholder is placed nearest to those other members with whom he is in greatest agreement and most distant from those with whom he agrees least. Once the matrices are constructed in this manner, it is possible to identify any blocs that might appear within the group. In the present study 60 percent of paired agreements with all other members of a bloc was employed as the criterion for inclusion.

---

[1] As representative works of these authors, see Stuart A. Rice, "The Identification of Blocs in Small Political Bodies," *American Political Science Review*, August 1927; Herman C. Beyle, *Identification and Analysis of Attribute-Cluster-Blocs*, Chicago: University of Chicago Press, 1931; C. Herman Pritchett, *The Roosevelt Court*, New York: The Macmillan Company, 1948; Glendon A. Schubert, *Quantitative Analysis of Judicial Behavior*, New York: The Free Press of Glencoe, Inc., 1959; David B. Truman, *The Congressional Party*, New York: John Wiley & Sons, Inc., 1959.

To reinforce the identification of bloc alignments as revealed in the general and chronological analyses of the 36 roll-call votes, two additional approaches were utilized. In the first, a matrix was constructed showing the frequency of paired agreements between freeholders when voting in the minority. The use of paired agreements in dissent is a logical refinement of the original methodological assumption. If bloc alignments are best identified in nonunanimous votes of small groups, they may be identified *a fortiori* by analysis of agreements in dissent from the majority in such votes. The bloc was defined in this case so as to exclude from it every member who did not agree at least once in dissent with every other member within it.

The second reinforcing technique employed was an analysis of only those roll-call votes where the blocs clearly opposed each other. Bi-bloc votes in which the blocs voted together were excluded from computation on the assumption that those votes might have distorted the percentages of paired agreements on all 36 votes. Hence, only those votes were considered which showed a majority of the district-bloc members present and voting on one side of the issue and a majority of merger-bloc freeholders present and voting on the other side. A total of 18 roll-call votes fell into this category.

The results of the two supplementary quantitative approaches described above verified the voting blocs previously identified in Chapter Three. Because of space limitations the two resulting matrices have been omitted. However, some refinements of the bloc analysis derived from these matrices are discussed on page 28 of the text.

As noted in Chapter Three, Freeholder Orchard was excluded from the quantitative analysis since he participated in only 6 of the 36 roll-call votes. All other freeholders took part in at least 22 of the 36 votes. Ten members voted in at least 31, and four freeholders (Buder, Deakin, Graham, and Simmons) particpated in all 36 roll-call votes.